W9-BSI-875

THE WORK
OF THE
CHAPLAIN

NAOMI K. PAGET

JANET R. McCORMACK

JUDSON PRESS
PUBLISHERS SINCE 1824
VALLEY FORGE

*This book is dedicated to the women and men
who have devoted their ministry
to providing spiritual care to people in need
on highways and byways as Christian chaplains.*

THE WORK OF THE CHAPLAIN
© 2006 by Judson Press, Valley Forge, PA 19482-0851
All rights reserved.

Anecdotes included in this volume are all taken from the personal experience of the authors. Names of persons, organizations, and institutions have been changed to protect the privacy of the clients.

Unless otherwise indicated, Bible quotations in this volume are from the HOLY BIBLE: New International Version, copyright © 1973, 1978, 1984. Used by permission of Zondervan Bible Publishers. Scriptures marked NKJV are from the New King James Version of the Bible. Copyright © 1982 by Thomas Nelson, Inc. Used by permission. All rights reserved. Scriptures marked NRSV are from the New Revised Standard Version of the Bible, copyright 1989, Division of Christian Education of the National Council of the Churches of Christ in the United States of America. Used by permission. All rights reserved.

Library of Congress Cataloging-in-Publication Data
Paget, Naomi K.
The work of the chaplain / Naomi K. Paget, Janet R. McCormack.
p. cm.
ISBN 978-0-8170-1499-5 (pbk. : alk. paper) 1. Chaplains. I. McCormack, Janet R. II. Title.
BV4375.P34 2006   253—dc22
2006017855

Printed in the U.S.A.
First printing, 2006.

CONTENTS

114789

INTRODUCTION

The Work of the Christian Chaplain

Chaplains and clergy share many tasks and competencies. Both have experienced a special call to ministry and service. Both are teachers, caregivers, witnesses of their own faith, and advocates for people. Both have a desire to equip people to grow in spiritual maturity. So what's the difference? Perhaps the greatest difference is the setting in which the ministry is provided.

Community clergy usually minister to a group of people who have like or similar religious beliefs and who share many common cultural identities—language, geographic location, socioeconomic status, or ethnic identity. Chaplains, on the other hand, usually minister to a group of people of many different religious beliefs or no religious beliefs at all. These people usually represent many different cultural identities, including those of education, profession, and political persuasion. Community clergy are given authority by a congregation or ecclesiastical body, whereas chaplains are given authority by the institution that *employs* them in addition to the ecclesiastical body that *endorses* them. And community clergy usually minister in a house of worship while the chaplain usually ministers in the marketplace—places not usually considered "religious."

Chaplains are clergy members from any one of various religious faiths who have chosen to minister to a group of people outside the walls of a church or other house of worship. They are usually employed by an institution or agency and serve the clients, employees, and families of the institution. From a Christian perspective, their role is pastoral, prophetic, and priestly, even while being nonreligious to those who profess no religion. They enter the ministry situation with no personal agenda and the attitude of a servant.

Christian chaplains are an extension of Christ's ministry to all people. There is a common misconception that chaplains have "left the real ministry" to do social ministry. This is far from accurate. Jesus did make a habit of regular synagogue attendance, and he often taught there (Luke 4:16-21, 44). However, most of his ministry was very much outside the walls of the institutional "church." He taught on the seashore, on mountaintops, over dinner tables, and along the roads as he walked. What's more, he did not limit his ministry to devout Jews. He befriended sinners and tax collectors, healed Romans and Samaritans, and preached to crowds of mixed Jewish and Gentile ancestry. Following Christ's example of cross-cultural ministry, chaplains provide many forms of caring ministry to countless people in various places beyond the walls of the church.

The pages that follow provide a wealth of information about the issues that chaplains face, the work they do, and the possibilities for many ministry settings and situations. From personal experience and a vast repository of resources, we offer information that will be helpful to those who are called to chaplain ministry or who are interested in such a ministry.

The purpose of this book is to offer insights into many different chaplain ministries and to clarify the nature of the work—the ministry—of the chaplain. It is our hope that this book will be a helpful resource and tool for pastors, students, chaplains, and laity who seek to provide effective spiritual care.

PART ONE

Foundations for Chaplaincy

CHAPTER 1

Historical and Legal Foundations for Chaplaincy

The development of chaplain ministry has its roots in ancient history. Religious men and women often accompanied armies into battle as priests. Chaplains sailed with Sir Francis Drake in the sixteenth century and fought with George Washington during the Revolutionary War. They have counseled and consulted for kings, parliaments, and governments—for the incarcerated, the sick, and the disenfranchised.

Today chaplains are found in many settings. Placement is limited only by a lack of imagination. Chaplains come from a variety of faiths, professions, and ministries. They may be laity—men and women who respond to God's call to provide care and compassion in their communities or organizations. They may be ordained clergy, counselors, teachers, social workers, or psychologists. Chaplains may also be full-time vocational ministers, committed to spiritual care through an institution.

Historical Foundations for Chaplaincy

The word *chaplain* comes from the early history of the Christian church. Traditionally, a story relates the compassion of a fourth-century holy man named Martin who shared his cloak with a beggar. Upon the death of Bishop Martin, his cloak (*capella* in Latin) was enshrined as a reminder of the sacred act of compassion. The guardian of the *capella* became known as the *chapelain,* which transliterated into English became *chaplain.* Today the chaplain continues to guard the sacred and to share his or her cape out of compassion.

Perhaps the most documented history in chaplaincy is in the area of military chaplaincy. From ancient times, chaplains have served the armies of the world. The Continental Congress recognized the need for professional chaplains and authorized salaries equal to regimental surgeons, thereby elevating chaplaincy to a professional status. Today, chaplains serve in all branches of the United States military as officers and professional caregivers.

Health-care chaplaincy has also been well documented from the early twentieth century. When hospitals were first created, they were usually an extension of a religious group who provided care for their own followers. Later, hospitals began to care for people of many faith traditions. In doing so, multifaith needs were identified. When physicians recognized the advantage in providing spiritual care in addition to medical care, health-care chaplaincy was born. Today many health-care chaplains in the United States are trained in theology, psychosocial development, ethics, and a variety of other disciplines through seminaries, supervised clinical training, and other highly specialized forms of learning.

Many other types of chaplain ministry have developed as an outgrowth of military and hospital chaplaincy. Industrial and workplace chaplaincy existed in seventeenth-century Massachusetts where religious instruction was required in many factories, mills, and worksites. By the twentieth century, workplace chaplaincy expanded into many new areas, including corporations and small businesses, racetracks and casinos, poultry plants and truck stops. As people identify special-interest groups that benefit from spiritual care, chaplaincy positions are created. It is fairly common to find chaplains serving agencies that provide law enforcement, fire repression, and emergency medical response.

Chaplain ministry developed because people needed spiritual care even when they were not in church (or their faith's equivalent) and especially when they were in a crisis situation. Today, there is much clinical evidence that supports the benefits of spiritual care—chaplain ministry—for people who suffer during critical events. This ministry was once initiated by employers, governments, and agencies. Today it is often initiated by religious organizations and the victims of critical events.

Legal Foundations for Chaplaincy

Although the United States Constitution forbids a national religion, the same Constitution protects the individual's right to the free exercise of religion. People have the right to practice religion in personally meaningful ways, but they also have the right to decline participation. Chaplains serve in a pluralistic arena—multifaith—and therefore, must provide the same ministry to *all* people in the identified ministry group.

Chaplain ministry has been challenged on the legal front in several instances. The primary legal basis for the existence of chaplaincy in the United States is the common denominator supporting the "free exercise" "clause" in the First Amendment. However, in the 1980s a Jewish army chaplain helped define the ministry of chaplains by clearly stating that the chaplain's purpose was to provide for the free exercise of religion for everyone in the command, not just the people who were of the same faith tradition as the chaplain. That is, chaplains provide the opportunity for everyone to practice, or not practice, religion as an individual choice and style. Today chaplaincy continues to provide for the spiritual needs of all people in a way that no other established religious group can.

CHAPTER 2

Biblical Basis for Chaplaincy

Although the bulk of this volume is intended for and relevant to chaplains of all faith traditions, the perspective and tradition of both authors is Christian. Therefore, we felt it imperative to include this chapter—for ourselves and for other Christians—to establish the theological rationale that Christian chaplains in particular have for providing ministry in such a unique way. What biblical examples address the mission and methods of chaplain ministry?

Minister to "the Least of These"

Matthew 25 concerns Jesus' teaching about the value of all persons—not just those who shared his ethnicity, culture, and religion. Jesus taught that if people wanted to be considered "righteous" and "inherit the kingdom" of God, they were to minister to *all* persons, particularly those considered the "least of these."

Many of the people who were considered the "least of these" are still with us. They are the homeless, the disabled, the uneducated, and the terminally ill. Chaplains are called to minister to the disenfranchised of society—the "least of these."

On the other hand, chaplains face the challenge of providing loving care to *all* they encounter—even those whose social or economic status doesn't seem to warrant help or those whose celebrity already commands attention or assistance. Other times the challenge is providing and demonstrating the love of God to those who don't seem to *deserve* care—the perpetrator of heinous crimes or the one who threatens the Christian faith.

> His biggest worry should have been whether or not his latest crush would say yes to a movie and pizza. He should have been arguing with his parents about cleaning his room or doing his homework. He should have been a *teenager* with all the implications of the label. But he was in jail—a criminal. He had participated in the rape and murder of three young women. He was *persona non grata*—the vilest of villains. Even his *friends* would not visit. But the chaplain came, even before she was called.

The Matthew text speaks to the chaplain of the innate worth of *all* persons, not just those who agree with their religion, share their culture, or look like them. Because we are all "created in the image of God" (Genesis 1:27), we are all entitled to, and worthy of, compassionate ministry and respect. No one is outside the love or concern of God (John 3:16). Chaplains follow God's example by loving and caring for each person.

"Go" to Those in Need of Ministry

A second point from Matthew 25 that resonates with chaplaincy is that chaplains are to take the initiative and seek out those in need of their spiritual care. Jesus instructed people to take the initiative and *go* to those in need, not wait for people to come to them—specifically to those who are "sick or in prison." Jesus didn't say, "so that they will become believers" or "so that they will attend synagogue" or even "so that they will see God's love through you." He simply said that a truly righteous person should take the initiative and go and care for "the least of these."

While it would be incorrect to put forward this form of ministry, which is the essence of chaplaincy, as *the* biblical model for ministry, it *is* correct to say that there is biblical precedent for taking ministry to the people rather than waiting for them to come to the minister. The significance of the pattern for *going to* people in order to minister is that it was common in biblical times, that there is a long-standing precedent for this form of ministry, and that it is not a new or modern delivery system of ministry that should be looked at with suspicion.

> The chaplain's office had every convenience—telephone, computer, coffeemaker, and bathroom nearby. But few people took time to walk over to the human resources department when they wanted a listening ear. So the chaplain practiced intentional wandering to be available to everyone in every place, from the shipping docks to the executive boardroom.

The act of initiating ministry interventions by going to those in need is in itself a clear demonstration of love and concern.

"Good Works" Must Accompany Faith

In Matthew 25, Jesus seems also to be defining *spiritual care* in practical terms—giving people food, water, shelter, and clothing rather than using specifically religious terms, language, or rituals. This alone does not limit spiritual care to practical needs, nor does it negate the practical *and* spiritual helpfulness of religious terms, language, or rituals. This definition simply elevates practical care to ministry legitimacy. Jesus understood that unless their basic survival needs are met, people are not in any position to want or appreciate being in fellowship with others, be it with like-minded believers or in any other social community. Likewise, people certainly are not in a position to care about matters of theology or doctrine—even their own *eternal* survival needs—when they are focused on their *present and physical* survival needs.

By a chaplain's very mandate to be involved in the crises of people's lives, regardless of personal religious convictions, the chaplain is often in the position of ministering to the basic needs of others. That ministry is not a "hook" to obligate the client to remain for the sermon or any other overtly religious teaching or service but a genuine example of the chaplain's own living faith. Ministry is provided without conditions and unrealistic expectations, out of genuine love and compassion.

> Floods and rain had destroyed the community. Disaster relief units had arrived, and chaplains walked around each unit, providing words of comfort and assurance. But the most important thing they seemed to be doing was handing out water, blankets, and directions to the feeding stations. Two years later a woman entered a small church in her rebuilt community: "Pastor, I came to church today because you gave me a blanket when I lost my house."

The chaplain must always exercise wisdom in choosing the appropriate ministry intervention for each situation. Attending to the basic human physiological needs of survival must often take precedence over evangelizing with the gospel message. Starving people perceive that they have a greater need for food than they do for religion, and no amount of religion will assuage their aching bellies. The cold, the hungry, the thirsty, the hurt— they find little comfort in religious tracts and platitudes. They need blankets and a place of physical and emotional safety. The "good works" of chaplains and other ministers often open the doors for faith. Jesus made ministry practical in order to make evangelism possible. James also made this point when he asserted that by our good works (deeds) others will be able to see that our faith is genuine (James 2:14-17).

"Keeping Watch" Is Ministry in Action

Another chaplaincy concept modeled for us in Scripture is what Jesus asked for and needed from others during his darkest moments in the Garden of Gethsemane (Matthew 26:36-45). Twice what Jesus needed and what he asked—practically begged—his disciples for was that they "stay" and "keep watch." No "doing for" would help him in that hour. Not even his closest friends, Peter, James, and John, could *do* anything for him—except to stay and keep watch. Keeping watch involves active emotional and spiritual presence in addition to physical presence.

There is a tendency to discount the ministry of *being with* someone as not constituting "real" ministry. If it *is* considered ministry, then it is often seen as less important than "doing for" them or "witnessing to" them. This appears to be especially true in the Western culture that values doing over being. In ministering to others who are in crisis, the one ministering will often lament, "I didn't know what to say or do. All I could do was sit there and pray silently."

> The chaplain had sat with many parents during the dark hours following the death of a child. On this day, the chaplain herself was the mother whose son had died. People filled the house with love and compassion. They fixed meals, answered phones, prepared lists, and ran last-minute errands. The exception was a solitary young woman who simply sat with the grieving mother. It was then that the chaplain understood firsthand that "staying" and "keeping watch" were valuable ministry—because those acts of presence had ministered powerfully to her.

Matthew 26 demonstrates that Jesus was asking for his disciple's presence. He needed his disciples just to stay and be with him! The chaplain, as a representative or stand-in for God, is privileged to stay with someone who is in emotional, physical, or spiritual pain, without trying to fix the person's problems, offer unsolicited advice, or recite religious platitudes. When people realize they are not alone in their time of suffering, the fact that the chaplain has not abandoned them may enable them to believe that God has not abandoned them either. It is amazing how often a counselee will remark to the chaplain, "I don't remember what you said. I know it made sense at the time. All I really remember was that you stayed with me."

> The events of September 11, 2001, were witnessed with shock, fear, sadness, and pain. Even two thousand miles away in Colorado, people were riveted to their televisions. The human resources department of High Tech Access requested that the chaplain "just hang out with our folks. Most of them are glued to the TV monitors, but could you just watch with them?" Nothing could fix or explain the events of the day, but no one wanted to be alone.

The ministry of presence is often undervalued. The sick wait for visitors, the lonely delight in company, and the fearful take comfort in companionship. The chaplain who is present—keeping watch—communicates God's assurance, "Fear not, for I am with you" (Isaiah 41:10, NKJV).

Recognize the "Unknown God" in Diversity

Paul's ministry in Athens in Acts 17:16-34 shows that one can be true to the commands in the Great Commission even when being sensitive to the pluralistic cultural setting of one's listeners. Paul's ministry style shows the importance of the timing and pacing of how that ministry is conducted, a tremendous concern and respect for those who hear, and an understanding of the difference in approach to believers and nonbelievers. The chaplain must recognize the "unknown god" in diversity.

There are clear lessons in Paul's ministry to the Athenians on how to be culturally sensitive when in a pluralistic environment—one unlike your own homogeneous group—and still remain true to your own beliefs. Compassion and respect for those encountered are paramount. Closely following those qualities are a good understanding of your audience, a very deep understanding of your own faith and beliefs, patience to wait for an invitation, and an ability to draw analogies from people's culture that illustrate your own religious convictions.

A chaplain must also cultivate a humble spirit. Even though the chaplain is a representative and ambassador for God, the chaplain is not and never will be God. As such, the chaplain cannot decide for anyone how to think, believe, or act—even Jesus did not force others to follow him. The chaplain must demonstrate compassion for all persons by sharing ministry in action first. Only when given an invitation may the chaplain share the truth of his or her own beliefs.

The biblical basis for Christians to pursue chaplaincy answers the basic questions of *why* chaplain ministry is implemented in such a unique fashion. From the mandates "to go" and to serve "the least of these," chaplains understand that they initiate ministry to all people, regardless of age, gender, ethnicity, or faith tradition. From the request to "keep watch," chaplains understand that the ministry of presence is sometimes the most important ministry intervention chaplains provide. From the mandate to feed, clothe, and shelter, chaplains understand that practical acts of service are an essential part of demonstrating faith. And from the examples of Jesus and Paul, chaplains recognize the importance of respecting differences in culture and religion, always providing opportunities for people to choose their own paths.

PART TWO

The Work of the Chaplain

CHAPTER 3

Ministry Tasks and Competencies for the Chaplain

The chaplain role encompasses many ministry tasks. This chapter will present various legitimate roles of a chaplain—not as an exhaustive list, but as the most common possibilities. Most chaplains must demonstrate at least a minimal competency in all these areas.

Minister — Religious

Across most religious lines, the spiritual leader of the community is considered first to be a "minister"—the one who officiates over the religious activities of the faith community. Likewise, the chaplain provides the religious functions that people expect from clergy. Often performing ministry without the physical structure of a church, synagogue, temple, or mosque, the chaplain may provide these religious functions in seemingly unusual places—offices, outdoors, disaster sites, homes, or public buildings. But to people who have never experienced "traditional" religious programs, these locations may seem appropriate for the religious ministry provided.

Rites and Rituals

Chaplains are often called upon to provide rites and rituals. These may include the celebration of marriages, infant dedications, christenings, and baptisms. Some chaplains lead weekly worship services and offer Christian Communion during worship to requesting individuals. They may officiate at funerals, memorial services, and wakes. Depending upon the chaplain ministry setting, other more atypical rites and rituals may be employed. The hospital chaplain may perform a "Blessing of the Hands" for health-care workers who attend to patients. The truck-stop chaplain may hold a memorial service over meatloaf and lemon pie upon hearing of a trucking fatality. The race-car chaplain may offer a team blessing in the pits as crowds wait for the signal to "start your engines." The disaster-relief chaplain may provide memorial services standing in the rubble of a building or home. These rites and rituals are often quite unique, characterized by the distinctive nature of each particular institution.

Ceremonies

When employees are not church members or regular attendees of any particular faith community, the workplace chaplain may perform wedding ceremonies for those employees. These weddings may be conducted in rented facilities that are often not the chaplain's own place of worship.

> Don was a law enforcement officer who had frequently interacted with the chaplain after fatalities or complicated arrests and over "coffee and donuts." He was getting married to the woman of his dreams, but his bride came with a formidable family. They could not agree on church or officiant. After explaining these concerns, Don and his fiancée asked the chaplain to officiate the wedding ceremony at a local inn. Both family ministers were invited to participate in the ceremony, and Don and his bride began to facilitate reconciliation with their families.

Many chaplains perform ceremonies as a regular part of their institutional ministry. They participate in graduations, banquets or buffets, dedications of people, programs, buildings, and equipment, and other ceremonies initiated by the institution. Law-enforcement chaplains may wear agency uniforms and serve during the graduation ceremony of a police academy by leading the graduating officers in prayer and inspiration.

Most institutional chaplains minister at ceremonial events, while some chaplains are known as "ceremonial chaplains." These chaplains usually do not have regular client contact or parishioners but are called upon to provide invocations and other prayers for particular ceremonies. Some of these chaplains serve the United States Senate, state legislatures, law enforcement academies, and at Arlington Cemetery. On a local level, these chaplains offer prayer before football games, Boy Scout banquets, and service club luncheon meetings.

Religious Witness

Chaplains also assume the role of a religious witness to their own faith and beliefs. Although techniques and methods vary among denominations and religions, chaplains also represent their personal faith tradition to the institutions they serve. As religious pluralists, they do not initiate a religious or evangelistic conversation, but by their character and actions—their presence—they begin the relationship that might open the doors for sharing their faith message. Because Americans enjoy the right to the free exercise of religion, proselytizing—intentionally trying to convert someone to one's personal religious faith or belief system—is highly unethical. Instead, chaplains find common ground for building the relationships that build trust and encourage discovery. Being a religious pluralist is not abandoning one's faith. Being a religious pluralist requires strength and wisdom for the chaplain who is faithful to his or her own faith and beliefs while being respectful and supportive of people whose faith traditions and practices are very different. The result of religious accommodation is peace and unity—a place where each person can experience the transcendent and the divine without compromise, resentment, or universalism. When asked, chaplains share their own spiritual pilgrimage and witness to their own faith.

Religion may be defined as the practice of a particular system of faith and beliefs within a cultural setting. Spirituality may be defined more broadly as the search for understanding and connection to beliefs and values that give meaning to a person's life. As a minister, the chaplain is a spiritual *and* religious provider. Chaplains provide the religious ministry that is attached to various faith traditions, but they also provide spiritual care to people who profess no religion. Through religious practices and spiritual connections, chaplains help people find meaning and purpose in their existence and all they hold sacred. For many, this "sacred" could be God, but it could also be the transcendent, family, nature, or community.

Many Protestant denominations do not have a "priest." However, clergy of all faiths periodically serve in the priestly role. They stand before the people and cry out to God. In much the same way, chaplains have the ministry task of being a "priest" for the people they serve. Some chaplains act as intermediaries between God and people who feel they cannot or must not approach God personally. These people may be angry at God or they may feel unworthy of God. They may never have considered God as approachable. They may be ashamed, embarrassed, afraid, intimidated, or physically unable. When asked, the chaplain represents an individual before God.

> Tom was dying of AIDS. He was alone, weak, afraid, and sad. Few came to visit anymore, or and when someone did, the uncomfortable visitor made excuses to keep it short. But the chaplain came, visiting without personal agenda or judgmental assumptions—just to be with Tom. "I was afraid to ask God to heal me—I've never been a religious person. Why would God hear me? Besides, I can't talk with

this tube in my throat—I can't even get out of bed anymore. Will you talk to the Man Upstairs for me, Chaplain? I don't expect a miracle; I just don't want to be so scared."

Chaplains perform many of the same ministry tasks as other clergy, but their audience is much more culturally and religiously diverse. The venue may be quite different and the ministry may be unusual compared to the traditional ministries of the church. The chaplain performs the task of minister by borrowing from many religious traditions and providing the freedom for people to worship, celebrate, and remember in personally meaningful ways.

Pastor—Spiritual Care

In deference to our nation's ever increasing religious diversity, the language of chaplaincy is changing. At one time the preferred term was "pastoral care." Later "pastoral care" seemed to be too Christian and therefore narrow in scope. The more acceptable term is becoming "spiritual care," and chaplains now work in "spiritual care departments."

The traditional "pastoral" role of the chaplain is comparable to the role of clergy in most religious communities. The English word *pastor* is related to the word *pasture*, which conjures an image of the shepherd who cares for a flock—especially in the Christian scriptures. Thus, the chaplain's pastoral role may incorporate many spiritual-care ministries that are associated with the care and nurturing of people and their relationships within an institution. These spiritual-care ministries could include the classic and contemporary approaches—scriptural instruction, interpretation, prayer, meditation, spiritual direction, presence, listening, and reflection. Regardless of the spiritual care that is provided, the chaplain's pastoral tasks typically include assessing need, offering counsel, providing spiritual care, and being a servant leader. Each of these tasks is described more fully below.

Assessing the Need

The chaplain meets new people on a regular basis. Often these people come with urgent needs and issues for which they have few or no ready resources. They may not expect long-term spiritual care, but they recognize their inadequacy in a particular situation. Before the chaplain can provide any ministry intervention, the chaplain must make an assessment of the person and the circumstance.

> Donna wandered into the front office of the Agape Women's Job Corps. She asked to speak with a "counselor" because she had "a lot of problems to deal with." The receptionist served Donna a cup of coffee and reported to the chaplain, "There's a woman named Donna here to talk to you. She says she has a lot of problems to deal with. Can you see her now? She looks fragile."

In Donna's situation, the receptionist had already made an assessment: "She looks fragile." Without making assumptions or accepting other opinions at face value, the chaplain clarifies the situation by doing an informal assessment. This assessment is made during the initial conversation by listening to the client's story. The assessment becomes a foundation for the ministry that will be provided. In this way, the chaplain's spiritual care becomes assessment-directed rather than merely an alleviating of symptoms. The chaplain may consider many aspects of Donna's situation—her physical health, her psychological well-being and mental health history, her employment and economic situation, her relationship with family and friends, her connectedness or isolation from religious or spiritual life, and the many aspects of her cultural identity.

What kind of "counselor" was Donna expecting to see? What kinds of "problems" is she dealing with? How is she currently dealing with these problems? How has she dealt with them in the past? Who or what has been helping her up to now? Are these real or imaginary problems? Is Donna's perception of the problem consistent with the chaplain's perception of the problem? As the chaplain begins to clarify the situation, he or she is more able to provide appropriate spiritual care. The assessment provides the chaplain with the opportunity to intentionally observe, interpret, and consider possibilities for ministry intervention.

Some assessments are formalized questionnaires that are designed to identify specific areas that may require ministry intervention. Some assessments are informal, relating to general concerns or needs. Other assessments determine acute needs, both physical and emotional, such as whether or not the client is suicidal or malnourished. The assessment process is an intentional way to evaluate the situation and determine appropriate spiritual care interventions.

Offering Counsel

The chaplain is often called upon to be a counselor for employees, clients, employers, and institutions. While providing counsel is helpful, the chaplain must clearly understand the difference between being a *pastoral* (or spiritual) counselor and being a counselor in the therapeutic or clinical sense. Some chaplains are especially gifted or trained in counseling. This is a bonus. However, if the client seems to need more than four to six sessions, a referral is probably in order (see "Referrals" below). Chaplains must maintain a network of good counselors who specialize in many of the frequently needed areas of expertise—marriage, family, and children.

Counseling in the chaplaincy is distinctive in that spirituality and God-consciousness are the basis for discussion and intervention even when religious language is not being used. The reality of God within the relationship of counselor and counselee encourages reflections about faith, morality, sin, justice, mercy, and grace. The pastoral nature of chaplain counseling enables clients and employers to consider issues confidentially from a very personal perspective regardless of what is "politically correct." Some people feel freer to speak frankly with a chaplain. Knowing that the conversation is confidential, some people are uninhibited in expressing their true biases and predispositions. In such cases, the chaplain has an opportunity to engage in meaningful dialogue and clarification about values, ethics, and morals. The clarification process also allows the chaplain to educate people gently about universal ethical values that are also consistent with the chaplain's religious beliefs.

> The job corps ministry was designed to give a helping hand to women who needed assistance in finding employment. "I get tired of people trying to take advantage of the system. This is confidential, right, Chaplain? We're a Christian organization, but it's hard to ignore the fact that almost everyone who comes in here is black or Mexican."
>
> The chaplain responded, "That may be true, but poverty and unemployment happen in all ethnic groups. Our Christian values teach us to feed the hungry and clothe the naked whoever they are. Let's take race and racial stereotypes out of the equation and think about how we can respect all clients as individuals while we encourage them to become more independent."

The chaplain who offers counsel from the spiritual perspective cannot remain neutral to the ethical problems of the world. Moreover, the chaplain must be faithful to the teachings and guidelines of his or her own faith tradition.

Chaplain counseling is typically short-term or brief counseling. Most people seek the chaplain's counsel for a very specific problem or issue. The chaplain clarifies options and listens to the concerns being expressed. Sometimes, talking about the issue aloud with the chaplain is the primary need. In other cases, the chaplain may suggest possible courses of action or help define goals and strategies as short-term approaches. An old French proverb suggests the counseling task of the chaplain: "To heal sometimes, to remedy often, to comfort always."

No one noticed anything odd when the chaplain made her weekly stop in the executive offices and sat chatting with the CEO. But this discussion was no ordinary chat. Fifteen hundred employees would be laid off by the end of the week, and the CEO needed some "counsel" from the corporate chaplain. "I know there aren't any miracles that will change the fact that I have to announce the layoffs, but I'd sure like to vent about this whole thing. I feel relieved about the decision, but I feel bad about it, too. I know it's gonna be bad around here. Got any advice, Chaplain?"

Providing Spiritual Care
The chaplain often "shepherds" sheep of other religious pastures. That is, chaplains often provide spiritual ministry (what we call "pastoral ministry" in the Christian tradition) to people in and out of their own faith tradition. In a very broad way, the chaplain assists in emotional support, physical assistance, relational reconciliation, and spiritual encouragement. All of these expressions of caring ministry represent ways in which the chaplain provides spiritual care for the soul—regardless of faith tradition, denomination, or lack of religion.

In fact, this function of the chaplain could be considered an umbrella that encompasses all the roles described in this chapter—minister, pastor, intercessor, healer. However, the most obvious act of spiritual care is providing help in times of need. "Help" may take the form of practical acts of kindness, or it may come in the form of "suffering with"—sitting beside the sickbed, listening to a story, or waiting for news (see "Being Present" below). The chaplain seeks to care for people's souls by making unfortunate situations more bearable by providing appropriate relief.

Retired almost twenty-five years, the only pleasure Jim had was fishing. But arthritic fingers and weary knees no longer allowed him to dig up the night crawlers he loved to use for bait. Today the chaplain was "checking up" on corporate retirees, and in Jim's case, that meant spiritual care through delivering a can of worms.

Being a Servant Leader

The chaplain may be a person of authority—a military officer, a departmental manager, a team leader, or a senior staff member. The chaplain may also be the person who has the most resources for spiritual care within the organization. The chaplain may even be a prominent figure within the organization, among the community, or in the public eye. Regardless of status or wherewithal, the chaplain must assume the attitude of the servant.

The ministry of care must arise from a servant heart—the heart of compassion and care. The servant leader ministers in such a way that the recipient experiences an increase in well-being—feels less stressful, is more able to cope with the circumstances, and identifies possibilities for the future. The servant leader ministers to everyone with the same humble attitude. Everyone receives the same special attention and care regardless of the benefit to the chaplain. The chaplain who expects special treatment or recognition because of his or her status, education, title, or connections will be sadly disappointed when it is not forthcoming.

Intercessor—Advocate and Liaison

An advocate believes in a person and lends support, backing, or sponsorship to that person. An advocate may promote a specific position, campaign for a particular outcome, or simply stand in favor of a certain result. Chaplains serve as intercessors or advocates in many situations—for the individual and for the institution—especially in unusual or unexpected circumstances.

Personal Advocate

In the Christian scriptures, when the apostle John wrote about the *paraclete* in John 14:16 and 1 John 2:1, he was describing the Holy Spirit and Jesus as advocates. The Advocate was a helper— someone who would advise, exhort, comfort, strengthen, encourage, and intercede. In fact, the Advocate was to be summoned alongside the person in the circumstances of judgment. In the same way, a chaplain advocates for a person when the chaplain offers advice, counsels, provides supporting evidence or testimony, or acts as a mediator on that person's behalf.

Some people are unable to set appropriate boundaries and care for themselves, physically, emotionally, or spiritually. Some are afraid to stop others from taking advantage of them. They cannot or will not say, "I cannot help you any longer" or "No, I do not want to have just one drink for old time's sake" or "I will not stay and be abused again." In such cases, chaplains advocate by helping those individuals say no. While chaplains cannot make the decision for people in difficult situations, chaplains can advocate for them by advising, strengthening, and encouraging them to appropriate a healthier or safer life.

Institutional Advocate

Advocacy for the institution has similar functions. The chaplain acts as an institutional advocate by assisting an organization in personnel issues. Clarifying appropriate action, suitable outcomes, right behavior, or proper protocol is a priority for all chaplains who are employed by institutions, both private and public. When there is a misunderstanding between employees or clients and the institution, the chaplain often acts as an advocate for *both* groups. In doing so, the chaplain clarifies issues, presents both positions, and often advises and arbitrates. As an institutional advocate, the chaplain helps the institution be sensitive to employee issues and needs while protecting the integrity and mission of the institution.

The chaplain may lead various seminars, in-service programs, or training events to educate employees, clients, or other personnel about institutional policies, programs, protocols, or procedures. In this educational role, the chaplain intercedes for the institutional need to *share* information and the employees' need to *have* information.

When institutions have questions about religious holidays, observances, or prohibitions, those inquiries are often directed to the chaplain. In a world of multicultural institutions, demonstrating cultural and religious sensitivity is more than being "politically correct"; it is essential for the well-being of everyone. The chaplain is often called upon to be the resident "expert," demonstrating cross-cultural competence as an institutional advocate. Most chaplains cannot become completely knowledgeable about all cultural differences. Therefore, servant chaplains approach cultural differences with humility, willing to learn and apply new information.

The chaplain intercessor also acts as a liaison between clients and institutions. One special circumstance is in the event of a death. Institutions often request that the chaplain make the death notification to the family or the employees of the institution. With specialized training, the chaplain delivers the news of death—*in person* unless absolutely unable to do so. Understanding the grief reactions and the process of grieving are essential to this act of intercessory ministry. Death notifications may be complicated by language barriers, cultural differences, the involvement of children or teenagers, or particularly unusual circumstances—criminal activity, suicide, deaths perceived as preventable, kidnapping, or terrorism. The institution calls upon the chaplain to be a calm presence in the crisis of death.

There is also a unique situation in which the chaplain provides intercessory ministry from "insider status." Some of these chaplains include military chaplains who are part of the administrative personnel of the institution, but they are also the peers of many of the people to whom they provide ministry. Similarly, the police chaplain who was once a police officer or the fire chaplain who was once a firefighter—these are chaplains who capably serve as administrative liaisons. They have "insider status." For some chaplains, the issues become complicated because their status changes from "them" to "us." The roles and duties are vastly different, and having "insider status" can be frustrating with such role confusion. For example, being a doctor in a hospital is very different than being a hospital chaplain. A prison chaplain who was once an inmate faces even greater challenges with "insider status." Can he or she gain the trust of former peers? Or even more important, can he or she gain the trust of the warden and guards? "Insider status" can be a blessing and a curse.

Referrals

Part of the way the chaplain often acts as intercessor is by referring people to "specialists." When people seem to need more than four to six spiritual counseling sessions, the chaplain intercedes by making a referral to a therapist or licensed professional counselor. When someone threatens suicide or has a history of attempted suicide, the chaplain refers the client to a mental health professional. If a client is an alcoholic, the chaplain may help the client enroll in a local chapter of Alcoholics Anonymous (AA). Chaplains advocate and intercede for people by referring them to support groups, advocacy groups, legal aid, and financial assistance. The servant attitude of the chaplaincy remembers that chaplains are not experts in all fields and in all situations. Chaplains must provide healthy intercession for people by referring them to specialists when it is necessary.

Referrals are a positive intervention in spiritual care.

Healer—Physical, Psychological, Spiritual

As a healer, the chaplain is concerned with a person's holistic condition—physical, psychological, and spiritual. Therefore, the healing function of chaplaincy encompasses key skills that address the whole person: being present, listening, encouraging, intervening in crisis, and teaching or providing information.

Being Present
Chaplain ministry has often been called the "ministry of presence." Presence is both physical and emotional. First, the chaplain makes a conscious choice to be physically present with the client. Second, the chaplain is emotionally present with the client through empathetic listening. Through presence the chaplain begins to build the relationship that eventually brings comfort to those who feel alone in their suffering or despair.

Some become frustrated with the ministry of presence. *Goals* don't seem to get accomplished. *Tasks* don't seem important. *Doing* seems secondary to *being*. Both the chaplain and the public may perceive that nothing is happening. But for the experienced spiritual care provider, the art of "hanging out" with patients, clients, victims, or team members becomes an intentional event that leads to providing a calm presence during times of stress or chaos. The law enforcement chaplain practices intentional presence—"loitering with intent" to calm, to build relationships, to provide compassion. The health-care chaplain practices patient presence (in both senses of the word!)—serenely listening to the same narrative of diagnosis, treatment, and recuperative concerns. The crisis intervention or disaster relief chaplain practices "non-anxious presence"—demonstrating no anxiety or panic about the bombing, about the flooding, about destruction left by fires, tornadoes, hurricanes, or tsunamis.

The ministry of presence often looks like standing around the water cooler, circulating among the people, sitting quietly with someone, or having a cup of coffee in the lunchroom. Presence may seem insignificant, but presence is the grace gift that chaplains bring to the human encounter. It is being available in spite of other commitments. It is being physically present even when the surroundings seem threatening. It is being emotionally present although the anger or fear is uncomfortable. Presence is the grace gift that accepts the client who seems unacceptable.

The chaplain probably won't be able to "fix" problems, but the chaplain's presence is a reminder that spirituality is a part of the ordinary and extraordinary activities of life.

Sharing the moment of crisis through the ministry of presence may be the most powerful and appreciated act of ministry performed by the chaplain. The care-giving relationship is greatly strengthened when a person never finds him or herself alone because of the chaplain's own presence—or because of the chaplain's assurances that God is always there.

The presence of God in the person and ministry of the chaplain empowers the client to healing and wholeness. Chaplains are ordinary people with no supernatural power of their own. But in partnership with the presence of God, chaplains bring calm to chaos, victory over despair, comfort in loss, and sufficiency in need. Chaplains practice the presence of God through prayer, rites, rituals, listening, the spoken word, the holy scriptures, and acts of service. Clients often perceive the chaplain as the "God-person" in their midst. The very presence of the chaplain reminds the client that God is very present to them. Chaplains share God's presence with clients even as they share their own presence and words of assurance—"I am with you."

> Standing in the dispatch room, the chaplain could see that people were anxious about the manhunt that was going on. Dispatchers were carefully relaying messages to officers in the field, administration was standing by with legal and the executives, and officers in the building came to hear—live time—what was "going down." The chaplain could do nothing to make the situation better, but everyone was grateful to hear the chaplain's voice of calm in the chaos.

Listening

The chaplain is a listener most of the time and a speaker some of the time. *Listening* requires many more skills than simply *hearing* words and sounds. To listen, one must hear the physical sounds; assimilate those sounds with words, facial expressions, and body language; integrate sounds, words, facial expressions, and body language into the present experience; and then give sounds, words, facial expressions, body language, and experience meaning and voice. The chaplain often listens as people "tell their story." The story may be an account of an experience or the catharsis of repressed emotions. The chaplain enables the client to share that story without fear of judgment in a safe and caring environment.

There are some basic ethical considerations that one must observe in being a good listener. Chaplains are not *entitled* to talk, counsel, or ask questions. Instead, the chaplain asks permission to engage in conversation or enters into dialogue through mutual invitation. Providing a sense of privacy demonstrates respect for the client, and maintaining confidentiality is essential in the ministry relationship. Unless legally required to disclose information, the chaplain is bound to strict confidentiality. (These issues will be discussed more thoroughly in Chapter 11.)

Through empathetic listening, the chaplain *feels into* the fear, the uncertainty, or the pain of the client. Empathetic listening is more than feeling sorry for the client. Empathetic listening involves personal identification with the feelings of the speaker and assures the client that feelings as well as words are being heard and understood. Good listening will include the unspoken messages and feelings, too. Most people seek the chaplain for good listening, not good replying. Sometimes, silence is appropriate. A well-timed nod or "uh-huh" may fit the situation and offer more solace than eloquent speeches. When the chaplain listens and understands the concerns of the client, the chaplain is better able to make sound spiritual assessments to provide caring ministry.

Encouraging

When people experience disappointment or crisis, they often respond with fear, confusion, or anxiety. During these moments of upheaval or distress, people need encouragement. A significant demonstration of healing ministry is providing encouragement through well chosen words and specific ministry action. When all seems hopeless, the chaplain brings the assurance of hope by conveying encouragement to a soul that is despairing. People who are suffering will welcome the chaplain who calls out, "Don't be afraid. I'm here with you."

When people face stressful situations—death, illness, broken relationships, vocational changes, and other crises—they often feel helpless and vulnerable. In these situations, the chaplain may provide encouragement by listening, dialoguing, comforting, and clarifying that which seems so confusing. Sometimes the chaplain may help the client reframe the event or circumstance into a less painful explanation. Helping the client take smaller steps to reach smaller goals is very encouraging. Assuring the client that fear, anger, sadness, denial, or relief are not abnormal feelings to have during times of stress is also encouraging—no one wants to feel like he or she is going "crazy."

The chaplain provides encouragement by meeting needs, offering prayer and spiritual guidance, promoting confidence, and finding the silver lining in dark clouds. Encouragement may be consolation, comfort, reassurance, or optimism. Encouragement is *not* a shallow cheering-up or Pollyanna device. Encouragement is providing hope when things seem bleakest and empowering clients to move forward to spiritual, emotional, and physical healing.

New Orleans Baptist Seminary was badly damaged by Hurricane Katrina. None of the returning evacuees could have anticipated the devastation they found. She was standing in the middle of a darkened room—black with mold and slimy with every imaginable bacterium—weeping quietly. "There's no hope to find anything salvageable," she sobbed. "What will I do? I have nothing left. There's no hope." The chaplain held her and wept with her. After a while, together, they sorted through the debris to validate the significance of her life and the magnitude of her loss.

Intervening in Crisis

Whenever people experience an event that disrupts their emotional or psychological balance (homeostasis) to the extent that their usual coping mechanisms fail, they are in crisis. They need urgent and acute psychological support. This support is called crisis intervention. The crisis may *seem* minor to some observers, but personal perception of the crisis will determine the distress experienced by the individual. A broken leg may seem like a rite of passage to a teenage motorcyclist, but the same broken leg may be the end of a career for a professional athlete. Thus, chaplains may provide crisis intervention for a vast array of situations—each one a crisis to the individual involved.

For most chaplains, crisis intervention will be dealing with deaths of loved ones, broken or damaged relationships, termination of employment, relocations, terminal illness, suicide, or financial crisis. Some chaplains will be dealing with the aftermath of tornadoes, hurricanes, floods, and fire. For other chaplains, crisis intervention will be dealing with line-of-duty deaths, terrorism, war, or criminal activities.

Crisis intervention begins with the ministry of presence and listening, as described above. Some key strategies of crisis intervention include ventilation and validation of the emotions, assessment of referral needs, defusing of emotional overloads, and problem-solving through clarification of possible responses and solutions. Other strategies may include reducing the threat and challenge of the event through cognitive reinterpretation. Spiritual crisis intervention may also include prayer, personal confession, or sacramental ministry. Crisis intervention is the ministry by which chaplains help people reexamine their belief and values as they cope with the difficulties of life.

Because chaplains desire peace and spiritual health for the people to whom they minister, they often experience a sense of urgency when facing individuals who are in crisis. But a sense of urgency must not overlook the possibility of serious errors. In a crisis situation, chaplains should never try to "wing it" without specific intervention plans. As always, chaplains should not proselytize or forget that some people don't *want* religious or spiritual assistance. When the crisis is physical, unless the chaplain is also a medical professional, making medical assessments or discussing medical issues with a client is unprofessional and exceeds the chaplain's expertise. On the other hand, chaplains must be cautiously vigilant and observant enough to recognize urgent stress symptoms and clinical distress (e.g., recognizing the difference between feeling "sad" and being clinically depressed).

In the wake of Hurricanes Katrina and Rita, thousands of people were housed in shelters. The chaplain was visiting with many of these who were waiting—waiting for medicine, waiting for diagnosis, waiting to go home. "I don't think they can cure me," said a man holding the hand of a little boy. Concerned, the chaplain knelt beside him. "Can you tell me about that?" she urged. "I can't go home to fix my house, got no one to send in my place, and what can these people," he waved his hand at the disaster relief team, "do for homesickness?" Unable to cure his homesickness or fix his house, the chaplain stayed to listen, assess for other needs, and simply be present to the pain and suffering of the homesick evacuee.

Teaching or Providing Information
In the Hebrew scriptures, the psalmist likened God's lovingkindness to the provision of knowledge or information (Psalm 107). Whether a person needs deliverance from captivity

(addictions, codependent relationships, or unhealthy behaviors), from physical or spiritual hunger and thirst, from ignorance or immoral behavior, or from illness or death, people of many faith traditions believe that God's word heals people.

God's word may be scripture or prayer, but it may also be the practical information that a chaplain shares with clients who lack knowledge or information. As a healer, the chaplain is often the one who provides necessary information about *how* to accomplish a task, *what* the possible options are, *who* the potential resources are, or *where* help is available. Many people feel stronger and more able to cope with the circumstances of life when they have the information they need to deal with the situation. If "knowledge is power," the chaplain empowers people to healthier life by providing necessary information.

Education and training prepare people for many eventualities of life. Chaplains teach and inform people about practical topics relating to emotional and spiritual health and well-being. Some of these topics might include stress management, conflict resolution, money management, premarital counseling, divorce recovery, cultural diversity, or grief and mourning. Chaplains may also be called upon to teach through leading worship or providing sacramental ministry. They may offer scriptural instruction or classes on various religious beliefs and traditions. Chaplains also may be required to teach student chaplains and interested laity about the many aspects of chaplaincy and spiritual care ministry.

The department had suffered public humiliation and outrage when the media reported that the arsonist was a member of the city fire department. Even worse, two firefighters had died in the recent blaze. After a structured crisis intervention process that included peer support, catharsis, and information about stress responses and stress management, a firefighter commented, "Man, thanks,

Chaplain. I thought I was losing it when I kept having nightmares and couldn't eat or do anything right. I thought I was going crazy."

Critical moments in people's lives are times of confusion and distress. Things seem uncontrollable and unmanageable. People have a desperate need to "take control of the situation." When chaplains provide necessary information, clarify confusion, and teach practical skills, they help people begin to control at least one small part of their out-of-control lives.

CHAPTER 4

Military Chaplaincy

Chaplains are found in many settings. Some have a long history of chaplaincy, and others are relatively new. Each setting possesses unique opportunities for ministry and unique issues and challenges. The next few chapters will elaborate on several chaplain ministry settings, exploring the background, certification and employment requirements, compensation, and job responsibilities. We will begin with an in-depth look at the oldest and most regulated form of chaplaincy—military chaplaincy. All other forms of chaplaincy have been modeled and legally legitimized on its model. The remainder of the chapters in this section will consider other settings based upon similarities and difference to the military chaplaincy.

Military chaplains serve in all branches of the armed forces—army, sea services (navy, marine, and coast guard), and the air force—and in all components within the military: active duty, reserves, and National Guard. Seminarians who are in the reserves or National Guard may serve as chaplain candidates prior to graduation and ordination. Military chaplains are also the chaplains who minister to and in various branches of the federal government.

Although congressional criteria and the demands of the political, social, and cultural landscape change from time to time, chaplains must meet basic educational, religious, physical, and federal requirements in order to serve in the military. Because each branch and service component of the military also has its own particular needs, each will also have some minor differences in qualification requirements. Exceptions can be found to most qualifications, particularly when the need for chaplains outweighs a ready supply, such as during a protracted or unpopular war or in underrepresented population groups. However, there is a minimum standard shared by all branches.

Credentialed Religious Leader

A chaplain to the military is *a fully credentialed religious leader* within a particular religious body who is "loaned" to the military as an "ambassador" of that faith body. The endorsing body, the Department of Defense (DoD), and the particular branch of the military to which one wishes to be a chaplain set entry-level and continuing employment criteria.

Chaplains are first and foremost representatives of their own particular faith group and must be "endorsed" by an organization (the religious endorsing body) that meets three basic criteria established by the DoD. First, the organization must have 501(c)3 not-for-profit status; second, it must have a current candidate for military chaplaincy; and third, it must have a lay constituency. Because the United States seems to be moving more and more away from strict denominationalism into a more nondenominational, interdenominational, or even independent religious movement, the DoD has authorized some "umbrella" endorsing bodies (e.g., National Association of Evangelicals, Evangelical Church Alliance, The World Council of Independent Christian Churches).

The DoD has set minimum educational and practical requirements that candidates must meet within their endorsing body prior to being approved as a chaplain for postgraduate military service. Educationally, chaplains are currently required to have 72 semester hours of graduate school work (with no less than 36 hours in theology) from an academic institution accredited by the Association of Theological Schools (ATS). (For more information, see Appendix A, under "Theological Training.")

In terms of practical requirements, prospective chaplains are expected to have two years of civilian ministerial experience and meet the criteria for "ordination" to serve as a religious leader within their endorsing body. As long as the DoD's minimum educational requirement is met, the endorsing body has the prerogative to define the requirements for ordination and endorsement within their own faith group. (See "Religious Requirements" in Appendix A.)

Commissioned Officers

Once a religious body has endorsed a prospective military chaplain as being fully qualified to represent their group to the military, there are federal- and branch-specific criteria to be met. That is because military chaplains are also *commissioned officers* serving in a tightly structured, legalistic, and hierarchically ordered system that is ultimately controlled by the United States Congress. As such, these chaplains must meet federal entry-level and continuing employment criteria for officers. These involve age, medical, educational and physical requirements.

For all branches of the military, a prospective chaplain must be medically and physically fit enough to serve—especially in the missions required of the particular branch in which the chaplain is commissioned. Although there are always exceptions based on needs of the service and prior service in the military, typically a prospective chaplain must be endorsed, commissioned, and accessed for duty at an age young enough to assure he or she could serve twenty years of commissioned service time prior to age 62. Chaplains normally are accessed (i.e., hired) at pay grade 02 (First Lieutenant/Lieutenant) which reflects a completed master's degree, unless there are extenuating circumstances.

Military chaplains are paid, not by their endorsing body or through a chapel offering, but by the federal government as their employer. Presently, chaplains receive the pay and benefits commensurate with their commissioned rank as officers and their total time in the service, including any prior service time. Like all military members, chaplains take an oath to serve their country and are "contracted" for a particular job and duration of time. However, the United States Congress can (and often does) change the rules of that contract and its benefits without allowing the military personnel (including chaplains) to renegotiate or terminate the contract without penalty. All congressional changes are seen, at least at the time, to benefit the United States. Many of those changes also benefit the military personnel (e.g., pay raises, family benefits, promotion opportunities, ending the draft). However, other changes impose additional hardships on the member (e.g., increased service commitments, decreased medical or family benefits, unaccompanied tours of duty, change in scope of what constitutes proper military duties). Normally, in order to receive retirement benefits, military members must serve for a minimum of twenty years.

Accessions

When it comes to accessions (taking office and being employed in the military), chaplains are considered "professional officers," as are doctors and lawyers. That means chaplains receive direct commissions as officers without the necessity of going to a military academy or an officer candidate commissioning program, or being in the Reserve Officer Training Corps (ROTC) during their undergraduate schooling.

Anyone with prior military service who has earned Government Issue (GI) educational benefits may use those benefits to secure a theological degree at an Association of Theological Schools accredited seminary. However, unlike the tuition programs available to professional officers such as doctors and lawyers, there is no current program to finance theological education fully for chaplain candidates across all branches of the services. As of this writing, some branches (such as the army) that have a greater need for chaplains do provide limited tuition assistance for seminarians who are commissioned chaplain candidates. In large part, that is a product of supply and demand when it comes to having willing chaplain prospects; some branches need more chaplains than there are applicants. Additionally, when certain groups, such as Roman Catholic priests or minorities, are underrepresented in military chaplaincy, incentive exceptions may be offered.

With no denominational quota requirement for chaplains at present, prospective chaplains are approved on a "fully qualified" basis from their religious endorsing body and a "best qualified" basis by the accessions board of the military branch in question. Being a member of a denominationally, racially, or ethnically underrepresented group is typically a benefit to a prospective chaplain. Having any prior military experience, including being a chaplain candidate while in seminary, is also helpful. Any experience above the minimum requirements, such as an MDiv rather than an MA, additional masters or doctoral degrees, or more than two years of ministerial or chaplaincy experience, will almost certainly gain points with the accession board. Holding additional training—such as some formal and accredited Clinical Pastoral Education (CPE)—or credentials—such as being a licensed therapist—might also increase one's chances for accession. The educational institution from which one receives a theological education is also sometimes a tie-breaker between candidates—for example, a seminary with a specific concentration in chaplaincy and a reputation for graduating solid, successful military chaplains.

A prudent prospective chaplain should make inquiry about the current accession criteria directly to the chaplain recruiter of the branch in which he or she is interested. Sometimes a candidate can obtain a waiver for particular concerns (e.g., a prior existing medical condition), and if those concerns are addressed prior to applying for employment, with the exception granted in writing, that applicant is more likely to be accessed. Just as any job applicant in any field should, the prospective military chaplain would do well to compose a detailed résumé and choose personal and professional references carefully in order to highlight anything that could improve the chances of being accepted.

Retirement and Termination
Both the military and the endorsing body have a say in retirements or termination of a chaplain's employment. Military rank is competitive and is usually viewed as an "up or out" option. If an officer is not promoted to at least pay grade 04 (Major/Lieutenant Commander) with a minimum of twenty years in service, there are seldom any post-employment benefits or retired pay. (To receive retirement benefits at pay grade 05 [Lieutenant Colonel/Commander], one must serve a minimum of twenty-six years; for pay grade 06 [Colonel/Captain] a minimum of thirty years.) Conversely, a military member can seldom terminate his or her contract with the federal government voluntarily, especially without losing retirement benefits. (The most common exception is when a congressional mandate to drawdown the number of forces in the military [often at the end of war] opens a narrow window of opportunity for a member to take an "early out" or "early retirement.")

If an endorsing body withdraws its endorsement of a particular chaplain for cause (legal or moral issues), thereby voiding a key qualification for serving as a military chaplain, it is unlikely the chaplain would remain in any other military career field, although in rare circumstances, exceptions have been granted. If the endorsement withdrawal is for cause, the candidate may not have employment opportunities inside or outside of the military—especially in ministry settings.

Chaplain Candidacy

Chaplain candidates are a special category of military chaplains who function as intern trainees within the military while they are full-time seminarians. The military criteria for being approved as a chaplain candidate are much less stringent than being approved for full-time or reserve chaplaincy. However, the endorsing body has first say on who represents it in this capacity.

Endorsing bodies often require only that a candidate be a member in "good standing" of their religious body. Such "good standing" is usually determined by the candidate holding membership in the local faith community and actively participating in that community's life. Participation is commonly attested by a letter of reference from the senior clergy and through an interview by another chaplain or representative of the endorsing body.

Typical military criteria for chaplain candidates are full-time enrollment (9–12 semester hours per semester in residence) at an accredited ATS seminary; approval (versus the more stringent "endorsement") by a DoD-recognized endorsing body; satisfaction of all medical and physical requirements for the branch of the military, and being young enough to graduate from seminary and meet endorsement and accession criteria prior to the upper age limit. Although underrepresented groups are actively recruited to become chaplain candidates, if there is enough room or money in the budget, few applicants are turned away.

The purpose of the candidate program is to train future full-time chaplains, as well as to allow all parties to ascertain if the seminarian would be a good fit for full-time chaplaincy. As such, there is no promise on the part of the seminarian that he or she will seek employment as a chaplain, on the part of the endorsing body that they will guarantee to endorse the seminarian, or on the part of the military that they will access the candidate in the future. There is, however, an expectation by the government and the endorsing body that the seminarian should *apply*—for chaplaincy and to the same branch of service for which he or she was a candidate. If any tuition assistance has been granted, there will be terms for paying back the tuition if the seminarian is not accessed or enters a different branch of service.

Chaplain candidates are usually commissioned as 01 officers (Second Lieutenant/Ensign) unless they have already been commissioned at a higher rank. Candidates normally spend two to three summers on active duty training at the respective branch's chaplain school, learning the fundamentals of officership and ministry in the military, and practicing their ministry skills on a military installation under the supervision of an experienced chaplain. During active duty, candidates are paid according to their rank and time in service, and personnel performance reports are written concerning their training. These training days will count toward the candidate's active duty commissioned service time for both pay and retirement purposes should they become fulltime chaplains. Some seminaries grant semester-hour credit for this training.

Active Chaplaincy Duty

Like most military personnel, chaplains are based at a *military installation*. As an institution, an installation is in every way its own self-contained community. It has to provide for the needs of its nomadic population who move from assignment to assignment with little input in where or what that assignment will be. The installation has its own mayor (the commander) and various businesses, including those related to the specific military units of service (e.g., ships, airplanes, satellites, transportation). The base also has its own police and fire departments, shopping centers (commissaries and exchanges), housing, restaurants, social and recreational centers (e.g., clubs, golf courses, pools, theaters, libraries), medical and legal professional services, and in some locations, even schools. Navy ships, when deployed, are microcosms of this same community structure.

By tradition and law, the military installation also provides religious and spiritual support to its members and their families (and oftentimes military retirees, veterans, and their families) through access to chaplains, chapels, and a variety of chaplain services—both specifically religious and generally morale boosting.

As credentialed religious leaders, military chaplains are called upon to perform all the rites, rituals, ceremonies, and offices of clergy in their faith group. While there is no charge for any of the services provided by a chaplain to an ID-carrying military member or that member's family, there is also no requirement for a chaplain to perform any rite or service to anyone simply based on military membership. Specifically, chaplains are protected from being required to perform services contrary to the faith group they represent. While a chaplain may be expected to perform weddings, he or she would not be forced to officiate at the wedding for a couple that is theologically unacceptable in his or her faith tradition (e.g., the divorced, the person with no faith commitment, the cohabitating couple).

By the same token, it is not unusual for chaplains to find themselves officiating at a memorial or funeral service for a stranger of a different faith. A Baptist chaplain might co-officiate a "General Protestant" service with a chaplain from a Presbyterian background. A Lutheran chaplain might lead an ecumenical service alongside a Catholic priest. Chaplains who are ordained as a Jewish rabbi, a Muslim imam, Methodist elder, and a Buddhist priest might participate together in an interfaith prayer service.

In an emergency situation, a chaplain may make rather different choices about his or her faith tradition and convictions than that same chaplain would in a routine setting. For instance, a chaplain who personally adheres to believer's baptism might be willing to baptize a dying infant if there is no "baby baptizer" readily available in the time of crisis. In such critical moments, often a chaplain needs to make a decision to answer the real need behind the person's question rather than give a full theological response.

When it became obvious there were no survivors, the chaplain at the crash site stepped up supportive ministry to the young airmen who now had the difficult job of searching for the remains of their colleagues and friends. "Chappy, what if we can't find a body—or even some parts of Tom's body to bury? Will God let him go to heaven?"

"I don't have all the answers of what God can or will choose to do," the chaplain answered honestly, "but I do know that my Christian belief tells me that in heaven we will be given a new body that is recognizable but even better than the one we had on earth."

"Thanks," the airman said, and visibly relieved, he returned to sifting through the debris.

Proselytizing and the First Amendment

While a chaplain is expected and encouraged to act as a representative of his or her own faith body, military members are protected by the First Amendment from unwanted or unsolicited religious pressures. It is expected that their religious needs will be provided for under the "free exercise of religion" clause. In other words, United States law prohibits the chaplain from taking abusive advantage of his or her rank, position, or circumstances to evangelize, proselytize, or otherwise coerce or influence a person whose faith is different from the chaplain's own.

This is an important part of chaplaincy, and no where is it more critical than in the military. This is not to say that chaplains may not share their personal beliefs and individual experience of God. Naturally, a chaplain's faith tradition may emphasize outreach and evangelism of the nonbeliever, and therefore efforts to evangelize the nonbeliever might be expected and protected as a legitimate function of the chaplain's religious endorsement. However, within the pluralistic and diverse military culture, the needs of the "client" must dictate the role and timing of such sharing—not the needs or wishes of the chaplain.

> Having been approached by a Muslim to arrange a Friday prayer service in the chapel, the chaplain arranged for services to be led by a credentialed imam and advertised under the official banner of the chaplain services. After three months of attending that service, a woman approached the chaplain and asked, "Why is your Christian God so accepting of women in the military and in religion when it is forbidden in Islam?" Because the chaplain had respected the rights and needs of the Muslim community, this woman was ready to explore the similarities and differences in their faiths' practices.

Unique Factors

Chaplains have the legal distinction of being the only military personnel who hold total, legal *privileged communication* for their clients (see Chapter 11). As a result, chaplains are often called upon to counsel, whether or not they have any formal counseling training or experience. Counseling may be related to spiritual and religious issues or to moral, ethical, and legal issues. Most often, however, counseling involves relational and work issues that would not typically require privileged communication, only confidentiality.

Chaplains are the only military persons who are considered to be 100 percent *noncombatants*—even doctors are expected to defend their patients physically from an enemy. In theory, this noncombatant status protects chaplains under the Geneva Convention Rules of War from being prevented from ministering to friendly and even enemy prisoners of war (POWs)—even if the chaplain is himself or herself a POW.

Another unique aspect of military chaplaincy is that, although chaplains are staff officers without command authority except within their own career field's duty section, chaplains are expected to advise commanders on issues pertaining to their specialty as religious "experts" and can thus influence a commander's decisions. This is especially relevant where there is a question about issues of religious accommodation. The chaplain is often called on to advise commanding officers concerning the religious needs and rights of an individual and the needs of the military and the institution.

> The chaplain stated respectfully to the commander, "Ma'am, it is indeed a part of the belief system for a Seventh-day Adventist to worship on a Saturday. If this were wartime or even an exercise where we simulated being at war, he would not be seeking your aid in this accommodation, nor would I be advising for it. However, since we (the military) are in a position to allow him to worship as his faith background dictates without jeopardizing mission needs or punishing others (since he is willing to pull a Sunday shift), my advice is to grant him his accommodation request."

Chaplains also advise commanders on the general morale and welfare of the troops and sometimes on the broader moral and ethical practices and policies of the military and of particular officers. In the past, chaplains advocated for and succeeded in canceling the early military's tradition of paying the troops in part with a ration of whiskey; helped to remove strippers from being expected entertainment at officers' clubs and military functions; and led the public cry from within the institution for equal opportunity and antiharassment regulations and protections. Chaplains have the privilege and responsibility to minister to persons within the military institution, and they also have the ability to effect change in the institution itself.

CHAPTER 5

Health-care Chaplaincy

Chaplaincy in US hospitals developed in the mid-1920s. To speak of US health-care chaplaincy in the twenty-first century is to locate chaplains both inside and outside hospital settings—although most care still takes place in a hospital.

Chaplains within hospital walls may be generalists who are normally assigned to particular floors for continuity. However, in this age of medical specializations, chaplains have learned to specialize as well. They may become chaplaincy experts in medical specialties as diverse as emergency care, psychology, oncology, pediatrics, intensive care, obstetrics, neonatal, reconstructive and cosmetic surgery, burn medicine, infectious diseases—and even acquired immunodeficiency syndrome (AIDS) as a specialty within a specialty.

Geriatrics is a particularly specialized specialty. Health-care-related agencies have evolved to meet the needs of a graying America. Sometimes these related needs are met within local hospital walls. Other times they are met in stand-alone settings that may or may not be related to a local hospital. Chaplains have moved into those areas as well. The two primary geriatric settings are *hospice and palliative care*—which exist for the terminally ill regardless of age—and *elder care*—which often includes ambulatory retirement homes, long-term care, assisted living units, and hospice care within an eldercare setting. With society's antiaging mind-set almost bordering on panic, plastic surgery, transplants, and bionic replacement parts are becoming more available, and these treatments and their recovery care may take place in traditional hospital settings, specialized clinics, and outpatient settings where chaplains may be found as well.

Training & Placement Options

Hospital settings often require extensive education and experience, as well as denominational endorsement for chaplaincy credentialing and employment. In contrast, hospice, elder-care, and other outside-hospital-walls chaplaincies are not yet as structured and regulated. Education and credentialing criteria for chaplains in those areas may not be as formalized. The prudent chaplain applicant will ascertain the specific requirements from his or her endorsing body and the desired employing agency as early as possible.

Health-care chaplains can serve in full-time, part-time, or *pro re nata* (PRN) positions, meaning they are contracted, on-call staff members who respond "as needed." Other chaplain positions in the health-care setting include staff chaplains, spiritual care department chairs, and specially trained and accredited Clinical Pastoral Education (CPE) supervisors who oversee both CPE intern trainees and CPE supervisors-in-training.

PRN Chaplains

Because these on-call, part-time positions usually require a minimum of just one CPE unit (400 hours) of clinical training, they are open to seminarians or partially trained local clergy. This includes individuals from underrepresented populations, such as Roman Catholic priests, Jewish rabbis, Islamic imams, or ethnic minorities. PRN chaplaincy is also well suited for fully trained and certified chaplains who desire flexibility or for retirees wanting to continue ministering on a part-time basis.

Staff Chaplain

This position in a hospital setting typically requires many of the same minimum requirements demanded of military chaplains: a theological seminary education, ordination, and endorsement. Unlike in the military, there is no age or specific physical fitness requirement, but most institutions will require a minimum of four CPE units (1,600 hours) or one-year residency. Another common requirement is that staff chaplains be board certified under the auspices of the Association of Professional Chaplains (APC), although an institution may accept a candidate on probation if he or she is eligible for board certification. This certification amounts to the standard chaplaincy employment credentials, two to five years experience as a chaplain beyond internship training, and a committee interview and recommendation to APC by a group of board certified chaplains (BCCs) at the state level.

Department Chair Chaplain

This position normally adds to the staff chaplain requirements proven administration and supervision abilities, additional years of staff chaplain experience, and perhaps a Doctor of Ministry (DMin). A department chair chaplain would normally work in a hospital setting and supervise the spiritual care of multiple staff chaplains, chaplain interns, and volunteers. Many institutions further require that a prospective department chair chaplain have accreditation as a CPE supervisor.

CPE Supervisors

There are three levels of CPE supervisors: supervisor-in-training (SIT), associate CPE supervisor, and full supervisor. Typically, one becomes a CPE supervisor following an intensive course of training and accreditation. Individuals pursuing chaplaincy as a CPE supervisor must first meet all qualifications for staff chaplains and then be accepted for advanced training as a prospective supervisor by a committee of accredited CPE supervisors. During the supervisor training period, candidates meet with a CPE supervisory education peer group as well as with their own accredited CPE supervisor.

When they are deemed ready by their supervisor or another committee—typically one-to-four supervisory training units later—SITs are allowed to lead a CPE intern group while being overseen on their own supervision of that group. Candidates typically lead this intern group on their own, but they may also co-facilitate with a certified supervisor.

During this hands-on supervisory training time, SITs are preparing their own materials to meet a CPE supervision committee in order to become an associate CPE supervisor. Once they have been awarded that title, they are allowed to supervise intern CPE groups without any formal supervision of their own, but they are often mentored by a more experienced CPE supervisor.

When they feel ready, associate CPE supervisors again go before a committee and seek certification as a full CPE supervisor. From application for supervisory training to full accreditation, the process of becoming a CPE supervisor can take seven or more postseminary and residency years—with many options for nonselection at any or all points along the way. It is the rare candidate who makes it through the various committees without one or more nonselections.

It is worth noting that even after achieving full supervisor status themselves, not all CPE supervisors are deemed skilled and knowledgeable enough to train prospective CPE supervisors. To attain the position of a trainer, a CPE supervisor needs his or her own proven track record of supervisory experience and excellence as a supervisor of CPE interns.

CPE Interns

Individuals interested in a CPE intern chaplaincy can receive training as a year-long residency or by the CPE unit (again, 400 hours), which is analogous to a typical 13–15 week semester. Interns usually work in hospital settings, but they may also train in community-based settings outside of hospital walls, including local congregations, police departments, sports teams, and counseling centers. Unless their seminary has a curriculum provision for CPE training during seminary, interns have to pursue their CPE education and training after their seminary course work.

CPE training is a requirement for many forms of chaplaincy and an expectation for most faith groups. CPE students seek internship training for various other reasons. For some, it is an ordination requirement. For others, it is an opportunity to improve trauma and grief counseling skills. For others, it may be a transitional setting between seminary and a ministerial vocation.

Employment Terms

Because the chaplain is an employee of the health-care agency, the cost of health care, patient and doctor issues concerning insurance, and related financial management decisions affect chaplains in a comparable degree with other health-care workers. As institutional administrators look for areas to cut costs, professional chaplains are often the first to be terminated since there is rarely a shortage of local clergy willing to visit their own parishioners or wanting to "evangelize" the captive patient audiences. This is notwithstanding the 1998 requirements of the Joint Commission on the Accreditation of Healthcare Organizations (JCAHO) whose accreditation standards require hospitals to provide for the spiritual care of patients in order to receive JCAHO accreditation for their institution. Not surprisingly, hospital administration often feels that untrained volunteer clergy are the easiest and least expensive way to meet those requirements.

A cyclic pattern often emerges in which spiritual care departments within a hospital setting first lose their training programs; then chaplain staffs are decimated until the spiritual care department ceases to exist, and perhaps only PRN chaplains or volunteer clergy are left to provide spiritual care. Regrettably, untrained but well-intentioned volunteer clergy are often found to be ineffective and sometimes damaging in a pluralistic and diverse technical institution for which they are untrained and ill prepared. Consequently, patient and staff complaints mount. When the din of complaints reaches critical mass, visiting JCAHO reaccreditation officials will document the complaints, and lawsuits may even be filed. This causes administration to rethink their spiritual care requirements and hire one professional staff chaplain to train and supervise all the volunteer clergy. When this proves ineffective or too overwhelming for one person, more staff chaplains are hired, thus creating anew a spiritual care department. Finally, accredited CPE supervisors are hired to recruit and train chaplain CPE interns and maximize chaplaincy coverage. This lasts until the next set of budget cuts threatens to begin the downsizing phase of the cycle once again.

Perhaps the only thing that saves the professional chaplaincy in such a setting is an administrator who has personally experienced the benefits of spiritual care. No amount of number crunching can ever capture the benefits of well-delivered spiritual care to persons in need. Once an administrator has had that experience personally, the chaplains on that staff are usually protected from downsizing as long as that person remains in charge.

Ministry Functions

Health-care chaplaincy is conducted in a diverse and pluralistic setting where the "client" did not go to the institution with the specific need or intent for spiritual care. The patient is a captive audience, often unable to leave his or her bed and vulnerable due to the hospitalization circumstances. Therefore, a chaplain making a "cold call" (an unrequested visit) must be especially sensitive to the needs and wishes of the patient as they relate to a ministry of spiritual care. Chaplains honor the "free exercise" clause of the First Amendment not only by refraining themselves from "evangelizing" but also by guarding against anyone else who might seek to proselytize or take unfair advantage of a patient in a vulnerable situation.

Health-care chaplains, like military chaplains, may perform all the rites and offices of a religious leader in their faith group, and they are often called upon to officiate at ecumenical or interfaith functions as well. They may function with a client's local clergy as an *ad hoc* spiritual care team or as the only clergy member the client knows. Because of the emergency nature of much of health care, chaplains in this setting may be asked to perform services they may otherwise not do from their own theological position or tradition. Any chaplain would be well served to have thought through possible scenarios and formed a plan before an emergency ministration is requested. As always, being available, approachable, nonjudgmental, and still representing "The Holy" by title and mere presence is a necessary tension of chaplaincy.

> Ali was born Muslim but had not been practicing for years. Now that he was in hospice care, he was rethinking the meaning of life and life after death. He asked the Baptist chaplain to get the nurse to turn his bed to face east, toward Mecca, and to help him hold his hand with the index finger raised as he smiled and took his last breath. The patient was affirming for himself that there was "only one God." "The Muslim, Jewish, or Christian God?" the nurse asked. "I don't know," the chaplain answered, "but it seemed enough to Ali that he and God were communicating with each other at long last."

As one who ministers within—and to—a health-care institution, a chaplain serves as a member of the interdisciplinary patient care team. Thus, the chaplain has a role in educating administrators, staff, teams, and the community regarding the relationship between religious and spiritual issues related to patient care and the institution.

Health-care chaplains are also intercessors and advocates (see Chapter 3). They advise and encourage people in the health-care system so they may be free to choose their own path, to make difficult decisions, or to establish personal boundaries that meet their needs and affirm their values.

She had been found in her submerged car in the river. There was no brain activity, but the paramedic protocol required putting her on a ventilator for transport. The ER doctor was ready to pronounce her dead, but her adult children refused to have the ventilator disconnected for fear of "killing Mom." The chaplain understood their fear as well as their faith. After a lengthy time of listening and praying, she helped the family to act on their faith belief that God did not need a ventilator to miraculously heal Mom, and that alive or dead their mother was safe in God's care and love.

The expanding need for health-care agencies and professionals to keep up with rapidly increasing medical technology and options means chaplains must be well versed in medical ethics. In some institutions, chaplains not only serve on the staff ethics teams but also lead those teams in difficult health-care decisions. In fact, chaplains are often expected to clarify critical value issues with patients, family, staff, and the institution.

Health-care chaplains provide spiritual care through the critical ministries of presence, listening, and dialogue with patients, family, and other staff. They help redefine critical issues and sort out misunderstandings. Through their participation in the mutual journey, chaplains help patients, family, and staff reevaluate values and beliefs that give meaning to life and relationships. As chaplains facilitate listening, they help all parties involved understand, integrate, and respond to the transcendent—even (and especially) in times of uncertainty, suffering, and pain.

CHAPTER 6

Workplace Chaplaincy

Workplace chaplaincy has a long and meaningful history in the United States. In the 1640s, it was being implemented by the Massachusetts Bay Colony for employees who were required to work on Sundays. Since then, chaplains have served tobacco companies, trucking firms, food-processing plants, auto manufacturers, beverage bottlers, computer corporations, and the media. By the 1980s professional organizations were being formed with the express intent of finding positions for workplace chaplains. The workplace chaplain may serve in various settings, providing the benefits of spiritual care ministry to people of many professions and occupations.

Most people spend more hours at their workplace than in any other single location. It seems reasonable then, that when people face crises or significant changes in their lives, their work will be directly impacted. Distress and emotional upheaval affect concentration, productivity, or working relationships. Some unique issues workplace chaplains may face include layoffs, restructuring, buyouts and mergers, retirements, downsizing, and difficult deadlines. They may deal with changes in supervisors or management, revisions to mission statements, policies, and procedures, updates in technology and equipment, and shifts in the economy, which influence organizational targets and goals. Chaplains also deal with conflict resolution, cultural and religious accommodation, and even workplace ethics.

Workplace chaplains provide spiritual care for employees during working hours and, when necessary, during off hours too. People seldom compartmentalize their problems. Work problems are taken home, and domestic problems are taken to work. The chaplain has a valuable role to play in helping workers to defuse before they go home—or to vent personal concerns before attempting to return attention to the job. The workplace inevitably benefits when employees are valued as human beings, not just "bottom-line" producers. Work relationships become more cooperative, and employers see a decrease in absenteeism and health claims as well as a general increase in workers' spiritual, emotional, and physical well-being. There are benefits at home also, where families are less affected by workplace stress if an employee lets off professional steam before getting on the train or in the car to go home.

Confidentiality & Neutrality

Chaplain ministry in the workplace offers the additional benefit of feeling "safer" for employees and executives than traditional employee assistance programs. Programs for such issues as anger management, substance abuse, domestic violence, or gambling are often perceived as having a greater possibility of negative career impact. Workers know that admitting to an emotional problem, health concern, family crisis, or moral and ethical failure could result in career development stalls, relational fragmentation, or even termination.

Employees can feel confident that in the chaplain they have an advocate who is neutral to the corporate structure who could listen, give honest feedback, and clarify *in confidentiality*. They need someone who listens without justifying the bottom line. They need to be affirmed in their feelings of doubt, frustration, and loneliness. When workplace chaplains can identify the need for employee affirmation and encouragement, they can become the advocates who comfort and support employees during times of stress without compromising the employee's position, reputation, or perceived emotional status.

The company had been dealing with falling sales, smaller profit margins, and a changing economic climate. Layoffs were inevitable. Scott hated his job, but he couldn't tell his wife about his unhappy work attitude because she was already scared to death that he would lose his job and they would lose their new home. He didn't dare talk to his peers or boss because he might be labeled a "complainer" and be the first to be terminated. When the chaplain stopped by his cubicle, Scott called out, "Chaplain, could I talk to you— off the record?"

Hope & the Personal Touch

During times of layoffs, failing economy, and budget cuts, business leaders are especially susceptible to discouragement and stress. They need hope. Without hope, there is no good reason to keep on keeping on. When leaders are hopeful, they give courage to their followers, enabling them to wade through anxious situations and persevere in times of uncertainty. Chaplains are very often ministers of hope.

The high-tech world of many businesses creates a vacuum for connectedness. A worker does business in six different countries, communicates with hundreds of colleagues without ever seeing their faces, forms partnerships, and closes deals without a handshake—all from the confines of a three-walled cubicle. In such environments, workplace chaplains act as high-touch people who build one-to-one relationships, intentionally focusing on helping people learn to reconnect to themselves, others, and God.

In fact, chaplains act as mentors in the workplace—guiding, enabling, and modeling healthy living and healthy working.

Mentors are different than business coaches who focus on the external qualities of performance and presentation. Chaplains are mentors who focus on the interior world of feelings, emotions, and values—those qualities that make us human—bringing light to issues and conflicts, clarifying values, and confronting immorality and unethical behavior. Chaplains join employees as they participate in the journey, not just the "event." Employees in the workplace need relationships with people of character, competence, and courage—filled with God's love and demonstrating God's presence—and a chaplain should be that kind of person.

Education & Training

Workplace chaplains typically have a seminary education. They are usually ordained and endorsed by their ecclesiastical governing body. These chaplains have also completed one or two units (400–800 hours) of Clinical Pastoral Education and have specialized training in various areas of counseling, including marital, grief, divorce, conflict resolution, and interpersonal relationships. Certification in critical incident stress management and suicide intervention are almost always required. Marketplace Samaritans, Inc., a corporate chaplain organization, requires other training and expertise, including death notification procedures, religious accommodation issues, workplace violence awareness and prevention skills, anger management skills, post-termination counseling skills, and education in state confidentiality and reporting issues, as well as in other legal issues pertaining to sexual harassment, discrimination, and ethics.

Usually, chaplains in the workplace are considered professional mental health providers. With advanced degrees and highly specialized training, they command a salary typical of most university professors. Depending on part-time or full-time status of employment, they may also receive vacation pay, medical insurance, and other benefits. Business cards, offices, phones, pagers, e-mail, and travel expenses are common entitlements. Within each specific setting, equipment and benefits may vary. Processing plants provide rubber boots, high-tech industry provides personal digital assistants (PDAs), construction companies provide hard hats, and manufacturing plants issue safety glasses. Just as law enforcement chaplains receive bullet-proof vests and fire chaplains are issued turnout gear (coat, gloves, helmet, and boots), the workplace chaplain receives the appropriate equipment to minister in unique environments and settings.

Ministry Tasks

Workplace chaplains provide many services to their clients—employees and the institution. Some of these services are typical in most chaplain settings. Other services performed by workplace chaplains offer more unique opportunities for ministry. Chaplains may assist with employee orientations or even help the company president or CEO with drafting special communications such as a "letter of condolence" or a "letter of concern." Chaplains may also serve as the company "expert" or consultant on matters of religion, morality, ethics, morale, and accommodation as these issues affect the company or the employee.

Homestate Industries operates seven days a week. Several Muslim employees were labeled "troublemakers" and "lazy" by their peers because they seemed to take more frequent and longer breaks than other employees. Management asked the company chaplain to intervene. After an open discussion with the Muslim employees, the chaplain was able to facilitate communication with company management that led to religious accommodations that also reconciled the other employees. Muslim employees were allowed to take their breaks (of the same duration as everyone else) to coincide with their required prayer times, and a room closer to the main plant was provided so they didn't have to walk as far to participate in their prayers.

In some businesses—especially manufacturing plants and construction companies—chaplains lead or serve on a "death notification team" in the event of an employee death while on the job. The workplace also presents the chaplain with many opportunities to represent the "personal touch" side of the company to clients and customers when the presence of a company chaplain might be appropriate (e.g., death of a client or a client's family member, accident, community disaster). In some companies, the chaplain also contributes written materials specifically tailored for company circumstances—articles for the company newsletter or self-help materials to address specific needs (e.g., stress management, grief and mourning, divorce recovery, anger management).

Overall, workplace chaplaincy provides continuity for people's lives. It facilitates mental, physical, and emotional well-being as a priority for living and working. When employees and institutions face crises or difficult circumstances, workplace chaplains are available and present to provide onsite support through confidential listening and caring encouragement. Whether an employee requests the services of the chaplain or the chaplain informally visits the employee at his or her work site, trusting relationships form and lives are enriched through caring interventions. The workplace chaplain brings spirituality, not religion, to the workplace— the opportunity to look inward, to clarify and live out values and beliefs in an appropriate manner while celebrating life and finding joy in work.

CHAPTER 7

Correctional and Prison Chaplaincy

Spiritual care to the incarcerated is probably as established as the institutions of incarceration themselves. This is particularly true in the Christian tradition, which has taken to heart the lessons of Matthew 25—visiting those in prison. Long before federal prisons were conceived, city jails had visiting clergy who intentionally ministered to the needs of people who have been incarcerated. As early as June 1886, a group of prison chaplains officially affiliated with the American Correctional Association, which recognized the value of religion and spirituality in the correctional process.

Today correctional chaplains are professionals with specialized training, representing their faith communities in the world of correctional institutions. They serve in many federal, state, county, and local facilities. (Some military chaplains are also specialized correctional chaplains.)

Education & Training

While the job responsibilities for correctional chaplains are similar to those of other chaplains, there are some key differences. For that reason, positions in correctional chaplaincy have educational and ministry requirements reminiscent of military chaplaincy. The Federal Department of Corrections requires chaplains to meet the requirements of *age* (less than 37 years old at the time of application), *suitability* (in employment, financial, and criminal history), and *physical standards* (pass drug tests and physical abilities test). There are in addition to the usual requirements of *education* (earned MDiv or the equivalent), *experience* (one CPE unit plus one year of residency), *religious credentials* (ordination or comparable status), and finally, *ecclesiastical endorsement* for correctional chaplaincy.

Not only does each correctional institution have basic qualifications and requirements for chaplaincy employment, but each state's department of corrections has set standards for correctional chaplains. Generally, most states have requirements similar to the federal standards. However, chaplains who are interested in a particular state's requirements should contact that state's department of corrections.

Correctional chaplains are often required to have additional specialized training related to suicide intervention, the criminal justice system, restorative justice issues, diversity within the correctional institution, and victimology. Prison chaplains are also well trained in substance abuse counseling and conflict resolution.

Professional correctional chaplains receive standard benefits of vacation, sick leave, and holiday pay, health and life insurance, and retirement and various savings plans. The Federal Bureau of Prisons ranks chaplains as GS-12 on the Federal Wage System. Salaries and pay scales vary according to locality pay tables, which are based on geographic area.

Volunteer Chaplains
The requirements for volunteer correctional chaplains vary greatly from one institution to another. In most cases, ordination and graduate theological education are not necessarily requirements. However, volunteer chaplains will certainly be required to submit to security and credit checks. They must also provide references from their ecclesiastical leader, and they must participate in the institution's orientation and training programs. Generally,

volunteer correctional chaplains are also required to be at least twenty-one years of age.

In terms of benefits and compensation, volunteer chaplains receive some supplies, training, and the thanks of a grateful correctional system. Some volunteers may be financially supported by a faith community or a religious organization.

Ministry Calling

Correctional chaplains provide spiritual care to those who are imprisoned and separated from their family and friends—from society in general. These chaplains also provide spiritual care to the institutional staff and to the family members of staff and inmates as requested. Jewish and Christian correctional chaplains may derive their sense of calling and vocation from the words of the prophet Isaiah (which Jesus claimed for himself in Luke 4:18-19): "The spirit of the Lord GOD is upon me, because the Lord has anointed me; he has sent me to bring good news to the oppressed, to bind up the brokenhearted, to proclaim liberty to the captives, and release to the prisoners" (Isaiah 61:1, NRSV).

Correctional chaplains provide the ministry of presence as they enter the world of locked doors, barbed-wire fences, armed guards, and painful solitude. They enter into the suffering of a defeated people who live with anger, depression, loneliness, hostility, and even despair. They penetrate the darkness of prisons while providing for the free exercise of religion for all inmates. In the tradition of Isaiah, they *preach* the good news of God's forgiveness and *restore* spiritual blindness. And while inmates may face many years of incarceration, chaplain ministry *releases* the oppressed from the emotional and spiritual prison of self-condemnation, anxiety, or bitterness.

Inmates suffer the same disappointments, hurts, and grief that others face on the outside. They experience separation, broken relationships, and betrayal; demotions, disappointments, deaths, and deteriorating self-esteem; physical illness or disease, emotional turmoil or distractions, financial or economic hardships, and spiritual crises. The difference between inmates and the average citizen is that inmates experience these things in complete isolation—separated from loved ones and support systems. The very nature of their circumstances makes them more vulnerable to emotional and spiritual distress.

> The judge had said, "Three strikes and you're out." Now he was in jail, awaiting trial. His mother was allowed to visit once a week, but for six days and 23 hours, he was alone. His friends had abandoned him, his family was ashamed of him, his church had lost contact with him, and his employer had given up on him. He had no one. The isolation and estrangement were like open wounds—painful and likely to bleed him to death. The chaplain's daily visits were like a balm on open sores.

Ministry Tasks

Correctional chaplains function in all the chaplaincy roles. As administrators, they manage religious programs and advise on many issues surrounding faith practices, providing opportunities for all prisoners to practice their faith as appropriate while honoring the right of others to practice no faith if they wish. Frequently, administration in this setting also requires coordinating and managing a pool of volunteers who minister to inmates. This may include recruitment, training, supervision, and evaluating the ministry being provided by volunteers of many faith communities. As a religious pluralist, correctional chaplains must encourage the participation of many religious traditions to meet the needs of the inmates.

Correctional chaplains are well known for their role as pastors and spiritual caregivers. In prison, this care may take the very practical form of assisting with letter writing, reading through difficult letters or documents, visiting families of the incarcerated, or sitting with a prisoner who is awaiting surgery, trial, parole hearings, or even death.

As ever, the pastoral role of chaplains is closely tied to their role as counselor. The goal of general (or pastoral) spiritual counseling is always reconciliation—to God, to self, or to others.

Prison chaplains provide many types of counseling beyond this general sort—including counsel related to marriage and family, grief counseling, religion, and even life skills. They allow the inmates to tell their story and be heard in a nonjudgmental atmosphere, paving the way for positive behavior by offering the opportunity to dialogue in an open atmosphere of neutrality and impartiality. In the pastoral role, chaplains are also called upon to assist in the notification of death or other tragedies—to inmates and to families of inmates.

As educators, correctional chaplains are often called upon to teach classes or facilitate support groups. They may teach seminars on grief recovery, stress or anger management, life skills, or conflict resolution. Depending on their faith tradition, they offer scriptural instruction, catechism classes, or discipleship programs. They teach inmates how to cope with their circumstances, prepare for employment, or get training or education for new jobs or vocations. In many cases, chaplains are also educators for the institution—teaching the staff and administrator some of the same skills.

In the correctional setting, the chaplain's role as minister may seem less critical, but many prison chaplains also have the opportunity to organize religious services. They officiate at weddings and funerals and perform liturgical duties as required by their own denominations or faith traditions. They provide individual and corporate prayer for inmates and the institution.

Correctional chaplains are also crisis interventionists. They provide a calm presence in chaos. As inmates experience bad news—rejection for parole, divorce, or other crises that disrupt their emotional balance—chaplains are called upon to provide acute psychological support. They may engage in suicide intervention or assessment of referral needs. When there is crisis in the correctional institution, the chaplain is often the reminder that God, too, is present in the chaos.

Finally, correctional chaplains act as a vital advocate for the inmates and liaison between the institution and the community of faith, raising awareness about the needs of the incarcerated and their families. They advise community clergy on matters pertaining to prison ministry and promote an understanding of how to assist inmates as they make the transition into the community after being confined. However, in their work with inmates and their families, correctional chaplains must be careful not to imply advocacy in terms of lawlessness, nor may they ever give legal, medical, or psychological advice.

Unique Factors

The environment within the correctional institution breeds many issues that intensify with the level of security of the institution. Jails, prisons, and penitentiaries all deal with inmates who succumb to peer pressure while confined. The pressure to conform to the attitude of "criminals" or "bad guys" is a coping mechanism for those who feel weak and vulnerable. The correctional chaplain is constantly dealing with the fear inmates have of being perceived as weak and exposed because they have chosen to make a lifestyle change, abandoning the life of criminal activity.

Inmates also deal with issues of depersonalization and dehumanization. They fear breaches of confidentiality, prejudice, and discrimination. For some, fear is the natural outcome of impending release, resettlement, or even execution. Correctional chaplains have the difficult task of building trust with inmates— through personalizing their relationships, humanizing their circumstances, equalizing their perceived inequities, and fostering peace and reconciliation in circumstances of prejudice, discrimination, racism, and all forms of injustice.

The environment of the correctional institution is often a microcosm of the greater world of crime outside the bars, guarded walls, and monitored rooms of the prison. Thus it is particularly vital for prison chaplains to understand the complicated nature of gangs, sexual assault, drugs, and crime. These are frequent issues inside prison walls, as well as in the world beyond.

Correctional institutions create acute vulnerability for chaplains. They are vulnerable to exploitation by experienced manipulators. They are vulnerable to showing favoritism to those who seem "nicer" or who demonstrate an interest in matters of faith. They are vulnerable to doing and saying things that may be innocent but that are interpreted or perceived quite differently—with legal ramifications. They are vulnerable to breaching confidentiality when questioned by those in authority or by those who seem casually interested. They are vulnerable to stereotyping, personal prejudices and biases, and exhaustion from intense, long-term spiritual care.

Correctional chaplains provide the context for spiritual health in one of the most difficult situations of life—a time of isolation and limited choices. Through spiritual care, religious services, and administration of rites and sacraments, the chaplain seeks to help the incarcerated person restore interpersonal relationships with God, with others, and with self. The chaplain seeks to provide hope to nonreligious and religious people by affirming human worth, the dignity of the individual, and God's forgiveness and mercy.

CHAPTER 8

First-responder Chaplaincy

First responders live in a world of high stress, danger, and uncertainty. Into the milieu of emergency services, we add the bureaucratic aggravation of policies, procedures, and chain-of-command. Further compounding the frustration are the personal circumstances of family, finances, and health. With all the typical concerns of anyone who works in the marketplace, a first responder faces the additional challenges of serving the public at large during unusual—and sometimes difficult—circumstances.

First responders include law enforcement, firefighters, paramedics, and disaster relief personnel. Many have chosen these professions because of the perceived control that is consistent with being *in charge*. On the job, the public expects them to take control of the scene and bring order to chaos. There is an expectation that first responders will do whatever is necessary to fulfill their duty—to complete their task. Consequently, many first responders have adopted the attitude of completely dominating the situation to accomplish the task. There is no room for error; the public (and the bureaucrats) expect positive outcomes every time.

There is unique culture of machismo among first responders that has nothing to do with being male or female. While this has been considered a negative masculine trait in some societies, first responders have adopted the very best and most positive characteristics of being macho. They have accepted the role, rights, and responsibility of taking control of many situations to protect or assist the innocent. They are internally motivated to take action, make quick decisions, calmly face danger if necessary, and assist others at all times. They occupy a place in the brotherhood and sisterhood that is the first-responder family—and no one messes with the *family*. There is great respect for order and chain-of-command as well a certain expectation of taking care of the professional family—sometimes at the risk of the personal family.

Ministry Needs

Personality, cultural machismo, and public expectation place great demands on first responders. They live in the tension of distress and eustress (good stress) that either enables them to function at peak performance or causes them to experience the physical, cognitive, emotional, and behavioral effects of physiological and psychological failure. Experiencing the most negative aspects of an unjust world in crisis inevitably cause stress and anxiety that many first responders cannot or will not share with personal family or others. They may feel compelled to protect their families from the negative aspects of their profession, or they may feel that they must live up to the hero ethos. The inability to ventilate emotions appropriately often distances spouses who do not understand the first-responder culture of machismo and who feel they are being excluded or distanced by their first-responder spouse. Consequently there is a higher rate of divorce and second-time divorce among this group than there is in the average population. This cultural climate requires great sensitivity and awareness on the part of first-responder chaplains.

First-responder chaplains include police or law enforcement chaplains, fire department chaplains, emergency services chaplains, or crisis and disaster relief chaplains. (Each of these will be described more fully below.) Their primary focus is to minister to the men and women who serve the public through emergency services agencies. As requested they also provide ministry to the families of first responders and to the staff members of these agencies. And by the nature of their contact with victims, they also minister to the community.

First-responder chaplains may also be known as public-safety or public-service chaplain's. In the context of public safety and service, chaplains provide spiritual care as a priority and also provide religious ministry, advocacy, institutional liaisons, and emotional and spiritual healing through presence, listening, encouragement, and direct interventions during personal crisis. Like other chaplains, they minister in a pluralistic environment regardless of race, national origin, religion, gender, sexual orientation, rank, or presumed guilt or innocence. Public-safety chaplains must remain neutral to the politics and operational differences that often divide agencies. They minister to all people in the department and to the many agencies that cooperate in emergencies, crises, and disasters.

Education & Training

First-responder chaplains usually fall into one of three categories: (1) local clergy volunteers, (2) paid professional chaplains, or (3) members of the first-responder agency who perform the duties of chaplain as collateral duty. Regardless of paid status, first-responder chaplains are expected to be professional in every aspect of their service to the agency, and with time and personal investment, they become family to the agency they serve.

The qualifications for first-responder chaplains (volunteer and paid) vary by department and agency. However, most agencies require some basic qualifications, such as a demonstrated call to public-service chaplaincy; ecclesiastical certification, recommendation, or endorsement by a recognized religious body; background and credit checks; and education, training, or experience in public safety and service ministry.

Many agencies require specialized training, such as suicide

intervention or critical incident stress management, ordination or license by a recognized ecclesiastical body, a seminary degree, specified CPE units, or a minimum number of years of ministerial experience. Some agencies may also require extensive interviews, 24-hour on-call availability, psychological testing, and a broad range of inventories including personality profiles, management style assessments, and conflict resolution methods.

First-responder chaplains must demonstrate emotional stability, flexibility in crisis, and a broad base of ministry skills. They must be a calm presence and demonstrate quiet confidence. Through humble service and compassion, first-responder chaplains earn the trust of those they serve. It is a well known fact that, from the first responders perspective, *people won't care how much you know until they know how much you care.*

Public-service chaplains must also be able to cooperate with many community agencies including medical facilities, jails and prisons, victim assistance organizations, and the coroner's office. The most successful chaplains seem to operate from the attitude of a servant, leading others because they are willing to follow.

Law Enforcement Chaplains

Law enforcement chaplains may serve municipal law enforcement agencies, such as city police, or county agencies, such as sheriff's departments. They may serve state agencies, such as the rangers, state patrol, or state police. Furthermore, they may serve federal agencies, such as the Secret Service, the FBI, or the US Border Patrol. In all such settings, chaplains may provide direct services to a particular station or office as well as being available to the rest of the department or agency.

Specific Duties
Law enforcement chaplains have many duties that relate directly to officers and staff of the law enforcement agency. For example,

they may ride with officers or accompany them on duty when requested; attend roll calls, staff meetings, and other departmental meetings; counsel officers, departmental staff, and families of officers and staff; visit officers and departmental personnel in hospitals, homes, and funeral homes; and even deal with alcohol or drug abuse problems.

Law enforcement chaplains also have many duties that relate to a victim or the community at large. In this arena, they may counsel victims of crime, disasters, or other major critical events; provide direct spiritual-care assistance to victims; make death and injury notifications; participate in suicide and hostage intervention; serve as part of the community disaster response team; and provide spiritual care for the homeless.

Finally, law enforcement chaplains have specific responsibilities to the agency they represent. They may provide ceremonial ministry at award ceremonies and graduations; act as liaison between the department and other community clergy; offer training in areas such as stress or time management, grief recovery, anger management, or conflict resolution; furnish expert information on issues of religion or ethics; sit on committees or review boards; serve on the department's critical incident response team; and provide referrals to appropriate agencies.

Respecting Boundaries
A successful law enforcement chaplain also observes the boundaries of chaplain ministry to officers and the agency. Chaplains must remember that they serve at the pleasure of the chief or ranking officer of the agency and that they are engaged to be *chaplains*, not "wanna-be" officers. Chaplains do not tell an officer how to do his or her job, interfere with investigations or crime scenes, speak on behalf of the department to the media, endanger an officer by endangering themselves, share confidences or evidence, preach to or proselytize officers or victims, or use the office of chaplain to avoid responsibility or threaten anyone. Chaplains

must know and observe all department policies, protocols, and procedure. They must be familiar with reporting procedures and radio communications. Duty and honor prohibit public criticism of the department, officers, or other personnel—loyalty is held in high esteem in this arena. Law enforcement chaplains must also maintain a life of integrity that is consistent with their religious faith. The officers will expect it.

Breaching the "Blue Wall"
Law enforcement officers are accustomed to meeting and working with people who regularly disappoint them or lie to them. They frequently work with people who have ulterior motives or who try to manipulate them to gain an advantage. Consequently, it takes time for the chaplain to build a trusting relationship with law enforcement personnel—to become part of the *family.*

One of the unique challenges a law enforcement chaplain faces is breaching the "Blue Wall." Neither physical nor visible, the psychological and social barrier that separates officers from the world is erected to insulate and protect. It is intentionally erected and judiciously guarded. Only the *accepted* are allowed entry. Because law enforcement offices deal with the most negative aspects of society and because they are constantly put under public scrutiny, they withdraw into a world where they are understood and accepted. The law enforcement chaplain only gains entrance when he or she demonstrates a consistent time commitment, a nonjudgmental posture in all questionable circumstances, an affirming attitude when criticism is the usual response, a demonstrated interest in the life and concerns of the officer and his or her family, and genuine acceptance of the officer in spite of differences, fallibilities, and expectations.

> Troop 9 Foxtrot was an independent group, far from head-quarters and dependent upon one another for support. Today the new chaplain was assigned to a trooper who

would introduce her to the territory. Twenty minutes into the ride and some juicy gossip about the troop, the trooper claimed an emergency, and dropped off the chaplain at an intersection to be picked up by another trooper. After a similar experience, she was picked up by yet another trooper.

Two rides later, a sergeant passing by noticed the chaplain standing at a rural intersection. After hearing a quick explanation, the sergeant laughed and asked, "It was a test. They want to know if they can trust you to keep a secret and if you'll complain when it gets uncomfortable or inconvenient."

Consistency of presence, complete honesty in all matters, and true humility—servanthood—will help earn the trust and respect necessary for meaningful relationships and effective ministry inside the Blue Wall.

Training & Education

Many agencies require specialized training for law enforcement chaplains. The first training topics deal with survival issues—physical fitness, burnout and self-care, first aid, CPR, and critical incident stress management. The second training category deals with procedural issues—radio communications, ride-alongs, death and injury notifications, traffic direction and stops, and chain of command. Another category might include interventions, such as suicide and hostage intervention, domestic violence, officer injury, or victim assistance. Law enforcement chaplains also receive specialized training in legal liability, judicial systems, departmental reporting, and testifying in court. Each agency has its own requirements, and even the experienced chaplain who moves from one agency to another may find that other courses must be completed before beginning the new assignment.

Law enforcement chaplains fill a unique role in providing spiritual care, religious ministry, and intercession in the lives of many officers and support personnel who serve the public in crises and stressful situations. Chaplains may be the only spiritual provider many officers and staff will ever know. With compassion, experience, and common sense, chaplains counsel and encourage through availability, presence, nonjudgmental listening, and building trusting relationships by being dependable, honest, and transparent.

Fire Department Chaplains

Fire department chaplains may serve volunteer departments in small towns or unincorporated areas. Alternatively they may serve large metropolitan departments with multiple divisions, including emergency medical services, fire prevention, and fire suppression, which can then be broken down into districts, stations, and companies. Fire chaplains may serve a particular group of firefighters or staff personnel at any one of these multiple layers.

Specific Duties

Duties of the fire chaplain are very similar to those of the law enforcement chaplain. Chaplains provide direct ministry to firefighters, departmental personnel, and family members of those individuals. They may provide counseling or visit the sick or injured, in the home or in hospitals and rehabilitation centers. They provide for spiritual needs through availability, presence, and listening, and they may even coordinate or officiate at family celebrations such as weddings or baptisms. They respond to alarms, drills, meetings, and socials. Fundamentally, their duty to the team is to be a *part* of the team.

> There were no words that seemed appropriate when the reports of death were received at stations all across the United States. Brothers and sisters had fallen in one of the worst tragedies firefighters had ever known. Manhattan

was far away, but in the greater family of firefighters, tragedy had impacted all. Fire chaplains reported to their stations because they knew that their fire families would be in distress. As prayers were lifted up, the chaplain honored those who had responded to "The Final Alarm."

Fire chaplains serve the department by serving as a resource to the chief on various religious and ethical issues; acting as a liaison to the community, churches, and local clergy; offering ceremonial ministry at graduations, award ceremonies, and meal events; making death and serious injury notifications; being a part of the interdisciplinary crisis intervention team; assisting as requested at accident scenes and fires; and teaching seminars and courses on such topics as stress and conflict management, life issues, ethics, and substance abuse.

Fire chaplains also provide direct assistance to victims at accidents scenes, offering crisis counseling and prayers as appropriate. They may be the first to assist a victim during the crisis of property loss, accident, or death. They may be the support and encouragement victims need as they wait for family members or others who will assist them. Many fire chaplains will respond to community disasters and assist victims in non-fire-related crises.

Last but not least, fire chaplains minister to the general community through education and direct spiritual care. Fire chaplains participate in community educational events as a representative both of the faith community and of the fire department. They serve on community crisis response teams, disaster preparedness teams, and other committees and organizations that benefit the psychosocial aspects of the community. They are mental health providers who bring a unique aspect of spirituality and spiritual care to the helping situation.

Fire chaplains earn the trust and respect of firefighters by their commitment to serving the *individuals* in the department, as well as by their loyalty to the department, their demonstrated honesty and integrity, and their personal faith. Through their availability, approachability, and intentional caring presence, fire chaplains minister to the perceived needs of firefighters and their families.

Education & Training

Fire chaplain candidates are usually expected to be duly ordained or licensed ministers within their ecclesiastical body. They should have denominational endorsement as a sign of their suitability for fire chaplaincy. Some departments require that their chaplains be United States citizens and have valid state-issued driver's licenses. Others may require proof of insurance or health fitness. Each department has specific requirements, and some requirements are negotiable under unusual circumstances. As in law enforcement chaplaincy, the primary requirements for fire chaplaincy are those of personal character and integrity. Credentials, education, status, and desire will never take the place of high moral and spiritual standards, compassion, and respectful acceptance of diversity.

Many fire chaplains are volunteers—clergy or laity from the community. Others are professional board-certified chaplains. Some work part-time and others are full-time employees of the department. Depending on budgets and ecclesiastical support, fire chaplains receive benefits and salary that are comparable to that of clergy in typical midsized congregations (250 members). Some fire chaplains work as missionaries supported by individual faith communities or their governing body. For others, salary is commensurate with rank—for example, New York City fire chaplains hold the rank of battalion chief.

Fire chaplains must be available (sometimes on a 24-hour basis) and willing to encounter situations under some extreme circumstances. They must be personally flexible and demonstrate professional and emotional maturity. They may be called to act as public relations officer after a particularly difficult response, and poise under public pressure will be expected.

Fire chaplains receive the same basic training that all chaplains receive. However, they receive special training in safety and fire suppression protocols. Because they respond during the event as well as after, they must be fully trained in department procedures and policies. Working with a high-stress population, they also have advanced training in stress mitigation, line of duty death, terrorism, and post traumatic stress syndrome. Each department emphasizes different aspects of chaplain services, but understanding the incident command structure, safety, and crisis intervention procedures will be universal priorities.

Fire chaplains are issued basic equipment after appointment. They will have standard turnout gear—personal protection equipment (PPE), including coat, pants, boots, gloves, and a helmet with "Chaplain" markings (usually a different color than firefighters or the chief). Typically, they also receive a chaplain's badge, business cards, and pager or cell phone. They are fully equipped to serve the men and women who serve the community.

Vocation & Calling

Although fire chaplains are not usually official members of the fire department (they are often volunteers), they represent God's love and serve the department. Many in the Judeo-Christian tradition are inspired to be the God-with-us depicted in Isaiah 43:2, which declares, "When you pass through the waters, I will be with you; and through the rivers, they will not overwhelm you; when you walk through fire you shall not be burned, and the flames shall not consume you" (NRSV). Chaplains are a reminder to firefighters and victims that God is present with them and cares for their safety and well-being. The chaplain is a friend, mentor, spiritual adviser, and spiritual caregiver. The chaplain is the link between the "hero ethos" of the firefighter and the finite human who exists behind the helmet and boots.

Emergency Services Chaplains

Emergency services chaplains may serve ambulance companies or search and rescue organizations. Many ambulance companies are private companies and not directly attached to a hospital or fire department. Some search and rescue companies are also private. Whether private or public, emergency services agencies often utilize chaplains to support their personnel.

The culture and environment of emergency services is very similar to the emergency medical services divisions of fire departments. However, they are usually much smaller organizations with fewer levels of hierarchy and management. The primary employees are Emergency Medical Technicians (EMTs), paramedics, and dispatchers. Usually dispatchers are based in offices and have no direct contact with victims except when they receive the initial 911 call—and as a result, unfortunately, they are often "hidden victims" of stress and delayed stress.

Unique Factors

One unique aspect of emergency services is the intentional brevity of the service. Paramedics, EMTs, and search and rescue personnel are concerned with safety and preventing further injury or loss. They do not expect to cure diseases or provide comprehensive treatment at the scene. They are trained to stabilize patients and transport them quickly to medical facilities for more intensive or long-term care. In doing so, their contact with the patient is very clinical and accelerated, and they often cannot recall names or any personal details about the people they rescue.

The stress these first responders experience is cumulative, and chaplain services to these people are usually centered on field support and stress mitigation after the fact. Cumulative stress often disables emergency services personnel through decreased cognitive functioning, relational dysfunction, and emotional overload. Chaplains are often used for critical incident stress management through debriefings, one-on-one counseling, and risk management.

Because emergency services are often about providing emergency medical assistance, chaplains must be aware of inherent dangers to themselves. Accident scenes may be dangerous. Often heavy equipment is in use, and there may be water hazards or medical dangers such as blood-borne pathogens, sharps (needles or scalpels), or high-voltage equipment. Chaplains with queasy stomachs would be wise to consider a different setting for ministry!

Chaplain requirements, duties, and issues are very similar to those of the fire department. However, because these agencies are usually small local offices, chaplains are typically volunteers or employees who do chaplain ministry as collateral duty. In such cases, chaplains may be exempt from some educational and technical training. Good listeners with strong stomachs may fit the bill.

Crisis Intervention & Disaster Chaplaincy

One of the fastest growing areas of chaplain specialization is in crisis or disaster intervention. Crisis chaplains are often employed by an institution and respond to community crisis as an extension of the institution's service to the community. Most chaplains respond to crises within their own organizations (the military, the hospital, the police department), but others respond to the general community during community emergencies. Crisis chaplains often serve multiple agencies and usually respond to the general community of victims during the crisis. "Victims" may include direct victims, innocent bystanders, rescue and relief workers, other first responders, and even the perpetrators of crimes (e.g., the arsonist who starts the forest fire, the drunk driver who causes the multicar fatality, or the terrorist who plants the bomb).

Specific Duties

Spiritual care in crisis is urgent, spontaneous, and finite. In most cases, victims have no prior association with the crisis chaplain and have no basis for trust or confidence. Furthermore, victims rarely have future contact with these crisis or disaster chaplains. Crisis chaplains prioritize stress mitigation through early intervention and cathartic ventilation—making the contact without delay and allowing the victim to "vent" reaction. Like EMTs, crisis chaplains have no expectations for providing long-term care. Crisis chaplains are, in effect, "spiritual paramedics."

Spiritual care in the aftermath of critical events and disasters is not necessarily "witnessing," "evangelizing," "preaching," or "proselytizing." During this critical period, spiritual care will be feeding the hungry, clothing the naked, providing water for the thirsty, sheltering the exposed, and caring for the wounded and sick. The practical acts of compassion and caring are the most immediate needs. Providing encouragement through presence, listening, and prayer (if invited) will be the most helpful interventions of spiritual care.

Education & Training

Crisis and disaster chaplains are highly trained in stress mitigation, trauma response, and victim psychology. Like other chaplain specialties, they are expert listeners and well acquainted with grief therapy and comforting grief. Previous education, training, and experience are the foundations for their ministry in this very specialized setting. However, contemporary global issues and political differences point to the need for supplemental education and training in providing appropriate spiritual care after terrorism, biological warfare, mass casualties, and other horrific disasters.

To minister effectively in community crisis and disaster relief, chaplains must familiarize themselves with the dynamics of relief organizations and their partnerships with other agencies. Many of these relationships are formalized through statements of understanding, but an equal number are informal agreements to "work together for the good of the community." There is no one organization that sets the standards for crisis or disaster chaplaincy or for endorsement to that chaplain specialty. There are, however, basic expectations for crisis intervention training that are common to most crisis organizations. The Emotional and Spiritual Care Committee of the National Volunteer Organizations Active in Disasters (NVOAD) has been active in dialogue and collaboration regarding the necessary "basic" training for spiritual care providers in disasters. NVOAD is composed of many voluntary organizations (American Red Cross, Salvation Army, World Vision, United Way of America, Mercy Medical Airlift, to name a few).

Two organizations have established benchmarks for crisis intervention training—the National Organi-zation for Victim Assistance (NOVA) and the International Critical Incident Stress Foundation (ICISF). Chaplains who enter the crisis or disaster specialty should complete the basic training provided by one of these organizations. Most agencies that endorse or certify chaplains in crisis intervention or disaster specialties require this basic training in addition to their own crisis training.

The need to formalize specialized training for disaster relief chaplains led to the creation of a specific training program, certification, and endorsement of disaster relief chaplains by the Southern Baptist Disaster Relief organization in 2004. Applicants must complete (1) an overview of the history, development, relationships, and philosophy of disaster relief ministry as a partnering organization in disaster response; (2) disaster relief chaplain training, designed to equip chaplains and other clergy with basic knowledge and skills to provide initial crisis ministry interventions; and (3) either the basic NOVA Community Crisis Response Team Training or the ICISF Group Crisis Intervention training.

82

Crisis and disaster chaplains are not usually *professional* disaster relief personnel; in other words, they do not receive a salary for disaster relief chaplaincy. They function as volunteer partners with disaster relief agencies and other critical response organizations during the period of crisis. They continue to be employed by their primary institution—the military, hospital, police or fire department, or corporation—and volunteer their time and expertise to other nonprofit relief agencies. In some cases, travel expenses are reimbursed by the relief agency, or the chaplain's institution sponsors the chaplain's temporary assignment away from "home."

Crisis chaplaincy received national recognition in 1998 with the formation of the Spiritual Care Aviation Incident Response team by the American Red Cross.

While the American Red Cross does not *provide* spiritual care, they do provide highly credentialed and experienced professional chaplains representing many faith traditions to assist the local community affected by the disaster. These Red Cross spiritual-care response team (SRT) chaplains are generally board certified chaplains who represent the various chaplain cognate groups (see Appendix A). SRT chaplains are administrative leaders who focus on helping the local community in *managing* the process of providing spiritual care within the affected community. In most cases, this administrative support involves organizing and supporting the actual crisis care providers. Most of the time, the spiritual care providers in this situation are local clergy and volunteers who arrive to minister practical and spiritual care to the community victims, first responders, and relief volunteers.

Unique Factors

Community clergy and laity who act as crisis and disaster chaplains are often the first spiritual care providers on the scene. Because they live and work in the community, they are the most available to assist victims during the disaster or immediately following the crisis. Often, they are familiar with the general population that is affected, have a network of resources established, and may even know the victims personally. The chaplain's familiarity with the locale and the people involved is an advantage for the victim but may cause complicating issues for the chaplain or other caregivers. The chaplain may face a difficult challenge if he or she must choose between ministering to a stranger whose needs are greater than a friend's.

In community disasters, the responding chaplain may also be a direct victim—especially if the disaster has widespread implications as in flooding, hurricanes, or fires. If the disaster chaplain is also the pastor or spiritual leader of a faith community in the affected region, there may be conflicts in the chaplain's ability to minister to the general population when parishioners are also victims. When the chaplain's family is impacted, even greater emotional conflicts are involved. The arrival of disaster chaplains from other communities is a welcome relief for community clergy and laity who act as crisis and disaster chaplains.

> Hurricane Rita left a path of destruction that practically immobilized East Texas. Rural communities had few resources to meet all the needs being expressed by residents. The pastor of one local church barely crawled out of his house alive, but he had a flock to care for and he needed to check on them. Two days later he returned home to find his wife and children gone—they couldn't wait for Dad to return to help them. They had gone to Auntie's house in a nearby town.

Important Survival Skills
Crisis and disaster chaplains are incredibly vulnerable at another level as well. They may feel the added distress of not having answers, not being in charge, and not having the resources to

"fix" the vast array of problems. They may feel the pressure of having to continue doing the daily and weekly routine tasks of being a parish minister while trying to minister to the needs of victims, relief workers, and relief agencies. They may have difficulty cooperating with leaders of other faith traditions within the community, or they may feel excluded by relief agencies who arrive to help. The media may intrude on their privacy or elevate them to unwelcomed celebrity status.

Such vulnerability leads to compassion fatigue. Crisis and disaster chaplains become emotionally depleted after hearing and experiencing the pain and suffering of victims. They are not tired *of being* compassionate, but they are tired *from being* compassionate. They no longer have the emotional energy to be present to people's stories.

Survival skills include basic self-care—before, during, and after the event. Setting appropriate boundaries, learning to delegate, and maintaining a personal support system are essential skills for crisis and disaster chaplains. Sometimes, these chaplains must self-select. They must be wise enough to excuse themselves from responding to the disaster. Perhaps they have recently experienced a death of a loved one or they are recovering from a serious illness or medical treatment. Perhaps they or their immediate family has been victimized. To be effective and helpful during the crisis moment, chaplains must redefine their own ministry expectations to accommodate the circumstances of the disaster and prioritize personal prayer, meditation, and worship. As the Christian tradition would say, they must remember to abide in the Vine (John 15:5).

CHAPTER 9

Other Chaplain Specialities

Campus Chaplains

Ministry on college campuses began with the interest of students who joined together in societies to nurture their spiritual side while gaining an education. In 1806, one of the most famous events in the history of student societies was the "haystack prayer meeting" at Williams College. Soon ecumenically organized Christian associations, led by laity, became the forerunners of campus ministry. The major growth in campus chaplaincy occurred following World War II with the return of hundreds of military chaplains. During these early years, campus ministries were overwhelmingly Christian and denominationally developed and supported. These campus ministers were typically led by paid, ordained staff members of local churches.

Most campuses these days, including church-related colleges and universities, have become highly pluralistic places with a developing need for trained, professional campus chaplains who are willing and able to minister to the spiritual and religious needs of all students, faculty, and staff. Ideal chaplaincy reflects an ecumenical or interfaith style in development of services, program, and personnel. Consistency with the kind of religious pluralism found in the interests and needs of the particular university community is essential. The campus chaplain may serve as the minister of the college chapel, but the chaplaincy serves the entire university population, not just the religious community on campus.

Education & Training

Campus chaplains to larger secular universities normally have an MDiv and endorsement or appointment from their denominational body. They may be full- or part-time employees of the university. The chaplain usually reports to a single academic or administrative office or to the council to whom he or she is responsible. (Typically this is the university president.)

The status of the chaplaincy within the university should allow chaplains to serve the entire university community. This status should also be reflected in title, position in the structure, committee membership—and appropriate academic preparation on the chaplain's part. Therefore, chaplains often possess faculty standing, even though the exercise of faculty responsibility is not always appropriate or desired. At smaller colleges, especially faith-related institutions, chaplains are usually appointed by the affiliated ecclesiastical body and may or may not be employed by the college. Credentialing for these small-college chaplains may be as extensive as that of their university counterparts, or they may be denominationally employed or appointed laity serving as "missionaries to academia." Many campus chaplains belong to The National Association of College and University Chaplains, Inc.

Specific Duties

Regardless of training, credentialing, or personal faith affiliation, campus chaplains seek to provide a place for students, staff, and faculty to connect to one another and to the greater community on a spiritual or religious level. Very close bonds commonly form between the chaplains and the campus community. A common thread within these bonds, regardless of doctrinal differences, is the importance of these connections themselves. The campus years are literally the years in which the students are exploring and choosing their future values. It is a time when they experiment with new ideas and behaviors as they test independence and adulthood. Often, it is also a time of great confusion.

He sat in the student center with his laptop and books scattered all around him. He had been so excited about college and getting away from home; he hadn't anticipated the emptiness or the sick-to-his-stomach feeling. As a tear threatened to give him away, a gentle hand touched his shoulder. The chaplain smiled, "How's the semester going so far?" Suddenly the student didn't feel so alone anymore.

Many students and faculty want an education that encourages them to bring their knowledge and skills to bear on political, moral, and social problems, to develop a sense of community where learning can take place, and to clarify some personal meaning in what they are doing and training to do. Campus chaplaincy is especially equipped to serve these spiritual, moral, and educational ends. Chaplains assist in the personal and spiritual growth of campus members and coordinate religious life on the campus. They encourage others to think and talk about faith; provide spiritual care and counseling on a variety of practical, moral, spiritual, and personal levels; and initiate and foster groups, coalitions, and programs that add to the quality of life in the university. Additionally, a chaplain is often called to help heal individual as well as corporate pain and suffering in times of trauma and crisis.

It was finals week and the Introduction to Sociology class had come with their blue books and pencils. At first they were quiet. When the professor was late, they began to whisper and make jokes. As the minutes stretched on, they knew something was seriously wrong. When the dean and chaplain came in to announce that the professor had been killed in a hit-and-run accident on the way to proctor the exam, the chaplain invited everyone to stay and talk or to attend the memorial service that evening after dinner.

Campus chaplains lead worship and scriptural instruction, officiate at ceremonies, and support students and campus employees by their ministry of presence. In particular, chaplains make themselves available to the wider university campus in spiritual matters, in direction and development, in issues related to life passages (birth, marriage, death), in relationship and career concerns, and in moral and ethical dilemmas. The chaplain also frequently serves as ombudsman (i.e., mediator) within the academic community as well as between various groups on campus.

A chaplain may also help with the more general needs of students. These may include assistance in securing off-campus housing, seeking tutorial assistance, or landing a part-time job. In each case, the chaplain may provide information or direct the student to the available college services. Wherever the campus community gathers, the chaplain will be there as a representative of the Holy One who cares about the whole person: body, mind, and spirit.

Sports & Recreation Chaplains

The very nature of chaplaincy itself, which takes ministry to the people of a target population, lends itself to a creative and entrepreneurial approach to ministry. Some of these creative chaplains provide spiritual care in resort and leisure settings, to amateur and professional sports teams, and in all types of recreational venues. Chaplains minister to athletes, spectators, and those involved in the sporting industry. Many become chaplains because they love a particular sport, they have "insider status" as an athlete, or they are workers in a sport or recreational arena.

Education & Training

The majority of these chaplains are volunteers who raise their own support in the pattern of sponsored missionaries, and most are willing to pay for their personal uniforms, licenses, and other requirements, for the privilege of ministering within a particular sport or leisure setting. Depending on the requirements of the sporting organization, chaplains may be professional endorsed chaplains, ordained clergy, or laity. They may report to a professional sporting organization, a chaplaincy organization specializing in a particular sport, the administrators of a sporting or leisure venue, or a denominational body.

Specific Duties
Chaplains in sports and recreation venues believe that God created humans with the capacity to get pleasure from the use of our bodies in physical activity. Athletic abilities, like all abilities, are a gift from God (Psalm 139:13-16) to be used wisely. Athletes gain fame and wealth, often at a very young age when they may not have the experience or wisdom to handle such notoriety. Chaplains have often found that athletes need and welcome spiritual care, support, and intervention—especially since a large public is in awe of them. Chaplains who have gained credibility by their actions are often invited into the lives of their constituents in a way that others would never be welcome.

> It was the day after the big game, and he was angry at the world. When you are responsible for the play that cost your team the championship, what's left for a fired, 28-year-old, washed-up athlete? Where were the fans now? When the chaplain came over, he just sat in silence until the athlete began to talk about his embarrassment and fears for his future. There was no resolution that day, but a suicide was averted and a young man knew he wouldn't have to be alone in his pain.

Chaplains minister to amateur and professional football, baseball, hockey, and soccer teams. They provide a ministry of presence to participants, fans, and staff of myriad racing venues—horse and dog racing tracks, drag and circle race-car tracks (e.g., NASCAR), and road racing and endurance racing (e.g., Grand Prix). Chaplains from the United States even care for the spiritual needs of the world's athletes in the Olympic Village.

Sports chaplains perform on-site spiritual care: chapel services, educational programs, work-related and family-related counseling, weddings, funerals, devotions, and always ministry of presence in the work and training areas where the sport happens. They pray over the athletes and teams before the start of sporting events. They seldom ask God to let their team or athlete win. Instead, they pray for safety, teamwork, fair play, and evidence of all of the training, dedication, and hard work that has been invested.

> The Special Olympics is a unique event for participants, workers, and spectators. Everyone is a "winner." This was Tommy's first event, and his family was nervous for him. "What could I pray for you, Tommy?" the chaplain asked. Tommy put his little hand up to the chaplain's ear and whispered, "Would it be okay to pray that I don't cry if I lose?"

Chaplaincy in resort and other leisure settings represents a steadily growing opportunity for ministry to people who work and play in areas all around the country. Resort chaplaincy is usually a multifaith form of counseling and spiritual program services available to people in resort business settings. A resort chaplain is equipped by experience, attitude, and training to offer spiritual ministry programs in resort settings for people of all religious faiths, as well as those who claim no religious affiliation. These chaplains typically have a personal affinity for and ability in the type of recreation their constituents enjoy. Resort chaplains may be found in parks, camps, and ski areas, at golf clubs, boating clubs, and RV parks, on cruise ships, and wherever else tourists gather to play and rest. One such ministry, A Christian Ministry in the National Parks, places chaplains in

United States parks during the summer to provide worship services and spiritual care to campers and park staff. It is an independent, ecumenical movement providing interdenominational religious services at sixty-five national parks, monuments, and recreation areas.

The niche-finding abilities of chaplains are virtually unlimited as many continue to turn their avocations into their vocations. Through spiritual presence, listening, and practical acts of caring, recreational and sports chaplains provide God's love to a world of athletes and people involved in many forms of recreation.

Parish Chaplains

Many religious and faith groups provide chaplain ministry as an extension of their religious body. Until the recent past, most of these chaplains were sent out by Christian churches and organizations, hence the reference of *parish* ministry. Whether the goal is outreach or community service, parish chaplains provide much needed spiritual care and ministry to the community. Regardless of background and previous experience, parish chaplains are usually volunteer members of a particular local congregation. In rare instances, they are part-time spiritual care staff members.

Retired professional chaplains (e.g., military, health-care, correctional) bring a wealth of experience, knowledge, and ability to parish chaplaincy. They understand the philosophy of ministering in the context of religious and cultural diversity and readily appreciate the right to free exercise of religion. They continue to do the same ministry they did in professional life, but now provide the ministry as a volunteer or part-time minister of the church. They no longer are employed by an institution "outside" their faith tradition, and they may appreciate the freedom to clearly represent their own beliefs.

Parish chaplains may also be retired clergy who are members of a particular congregation, denomination, or sect. They, too, bring a wealth of experience, knowledge, and pastoral ability to this role. Of course, for clergy who have limited experience ministering to people outside of their own faith tradition or congregation, there are new challenges and issues to face. Unlike in the congregations they once served, parish chaplains may not have well developed personal relationships with the people in the community environment. The community may represent diverse cultural and religious traditions and fail to welcome the chaplain who calls on them.

Some retired clergy who serve as parish chaplains may become frustrated that they are no longer the spiritual and congregational authority for the people they serve. They may not be called upon to preach, lead studies in their own sacred scriptures, or conduct the traditional rites of their faith. Instead, they will be called upon to provide many ceremonial services—the invocation at Boy Scout banquets, football games, baccalaureate services, or service club meetings. They may also be called upon to provide disaster relief or to offer support at the scene of an accident.

Parish chaplains may also be members of the laity. They minister in the community as volunteer chaplains in many of the settings we have already presented. They may be volunteer hospital or nursing home chaplains, law enforcement or fire department chaplains, or chaplains at resorts, campgrounds, and college campuses. Many of the chaplains who serve in disaster relief and victim assistance are also well-trained laity.

Typically, lay parish chaplains have received specialized training by their ecclesiastical body in the area of spiritual care—grief counseling, listening skills, stress mitigation, group facilitation, and pastoral counseling. They usually do not require endorsement from a religious body but are accountable to senior clergy or a specific congregational committee. Their responsibilities are often dictated by the institution they serve. They may be expected to visit clients four to eight hours a week or just twice a month. Each institution or agency will specify its expectations as to time commitment, services, and locations.

> The nursing home welcomed the weekly visits of the parish chaplain. She was associate pastor of a local church and often visited other patients when she visited her congregants in the home. She also provided weekly Bible studies and worship services and encouraged staff members and other personnel. She reported her activities to the church council and collaborated with the activities director of the nursing home. The multidisciplinary assessment team valued her observations of the emotional and spiritual conditions of the patients. Family members were relieved to call on her when there was no family clergy to conduct the funeral or officiate the memorial service. Parish chaplaincy was a lot like being the pastor of a multifaith church, and the nursing home was the congregation.

Parish chaplains serve in many nonprofit organizations. They may be chaplains in homeless shelters, rescue missions, halfway houses, evacuation centers, or battered women's shelters. They minister to clients at job corps, thrift stores, and teenage hangouts. Their responsibilities are often centered on being present and available for spiritual counseling and crisis intervention. They mentor and disciple; they guide and they lead. They do spiritual assessments, provide encouragement, and often do referrals to specialized agencies or care providers. They advocate and intercede for many of the disenfranchised people in society, and in all these functions, they fill a vital need for spiritual care in the community.

PART THREE

The Person of the Chaplain

CHAPTER 10

Keeping the Chaplain Accountable

Chaplains minister in the context of complicated issues and potentially compromising situations. According to their institutional expectations, individual faith and beliefs, professional standards, legal statutes, and personal ethics, chaplains maintain accountability to others and to themselves. Chaplain vulnerability is minimized when proactive steps are taken to protect chaplains, their clients, and the institutions they represent.

Institutional Accountability

When a person accepts an institutional position as a chaplain, he or she is making an explicit commitment to abide by the policies and procedures of that institution. The rules and expectations are quite clear, and there are few ambiguities. Challenging or disregarding those expectations could result in termination, fines, or criminal charges.

Leadership and administrative policies may create accountability through processes that provide supervision to help the chaplain stay on track. Regular meetings, reviews, and evaluations are routine practices for maintaining accountability, even though filing reports and meeting deadlines may be the most painful accountability structure that chaplains endure.

Another approach to institutional accountability is the multidisciplinary peer review. Chaplains dialogue with their peers within the institution to process difficult situations, evaluate interventions, and assess effectiveness. In some cases, peer reviews are used to discipline chaplains for unethical or questionable practices, or for incompetence. For example, a chaplain who seeks board certification may appear before a peer review board. A peer review board that finds a chaplain unsuitable or lacking in essential skills may cause the certification process to be delayed or terminated. In most cases, the peer review board would establish a process by which the applying chaplain would be mentored or have opportunity to address appropriately the issues that were raised.

When implicit expectations such as a proscription against cohabitation, the use of obscene language, or excessive alcohol consumption are challenged, the chaplain is accountable first to God and then to his or her own conscience. Few institutions can or will dictate morality, but many will implement sanctions against breaches in institutional, industrial, or professional ethics. Where there is doubt, the chaplain would do well to utilize good chaplain skills, such as clarification and self-examination.

Ecclesiastical Accountability

Chaplains do not minister in a vacuum. They are members of a specific religious body and are affiliated with a denomination or other faith group. In most cases, they are endorsed by their faith group to the institution in which they are providing ministry. As a representative of their religious faith and endorsing body, chaplains are held accountable for their beliefs and religious practices. When the chaplain's actions and words conflict with the teachings of the faith group, various forms of discipline may occur. The confrontation may be as simple as a meeting to discuss and advise, or it may be as severe as excommunication or revocation of the endorsement to chaplain ministry. In most faith groups, the ecclesiastical body provides a pastoral review committee that meets with the chaplain on a regular basis for support, evaluation, and

review. Proactive accountability is much healthier than ultima-
tums, censures, or reprimands. All chaplains must honor God and
obey the tenets of their faith.

Professional Accountability

Some chaplains are members of organizations such as the
Association of Professional Chaplains, the National Association
of Catholic Chaplains, or the American Association of Christian
Counselors. Each group has a code of ethics for chaplains and
other member professionals. Membership or certification by these
organizations requires the chaplain to support or endorse their
mission and principle, and to agree to abide by those standards.

Chaplains are held accountable by these organizations through
their membership and by participating in various activities within the organization. Some professional organizations require an
associate membership period during which chaplains are mentored or supervised. Some require and provide continuing education opportunities on the national and local levels to improve
skills, provide experiential learning, or develop knowledge in
new or focus areas. Some provide peer reviews that offer consul-
tation and counsel from peers in the field of chaplaincy. Others
provide an avenue for networking, career assessment, and personal therapy. Professional organizations provide healthy
accountability for chaplains while encouraging spiritual growth,
professional advancement, and academic instruction.

Legal Accountability

The United States Constitution provides some very specific guidance for chaplain accountability: "Congress shall make no law
respecting an establishment of religion, or prohibiting the free
exercise thereof; or abridging the freedom of speech, or of the
press; or the right of the people peaceably to assemble, and to

petition the Government for a redress of grievances." This First Amendment provides that there will be no national religion *established* and that all people are *free to exercise* religion or to *not* exercise religion. These mandates clearly establish that chaplains must provide equal ministry to all people who desire it, not just the people who embrace the same beliefs as the chaplain. The First Amendment and the United States Constitution are written to protect the individual citizen, not the chaplain's faith group or the institution in which he or she serves. Therefore, the chaplain is directly accountable to the United States Constitution.

The chaplain is also accountable to international treaties or conventions to which the United States has agreed. For example, chaplains may choose to minister to friendly and enemy prisoners of war, even if they are captured themselves. (Chaplains are not considered prisoners of war.) In this case, an international agreement, the Geneva Convention, provides the latitude that allows the detaining military power to direct the activities of a captured chaplain without later consequences to the chaplain from his or her government or religious endorsing body. The chaplain is expected to follow all orders for the sake of efficient function except in the case of conflict to professional conscience or sacerdotal mission.

Federal statutes and state regulations also provide accountability for chaplains. For example, the Health Insurance Portability and Accountability Act of 1996 (HIPAA) included privacy rules that created national standards to give patients increased control over protecting their health information. The chaplain is accountable to this statute in safeguarding a client's health information. Other statutes make the chaplain accountable for reporting child abuse, intent to commit suicide or homicide, or elder neglect and abuse to the proper authorities.

The federal Child Abuse Prevention and Treatment Act (CAPTA) passed in 1974 established the basis for all fifty states to pass laws mandating the reporting of child abuse and neglect. Each state defines mandated reporters differently. Clergy are not always specifically listed. However, most state laws define mandated reporters as anyone who while functioning in normal professional duties, comes into contact with persons who are abused, neglected, or intending to commit harm to self or others. Chaplains must know the laws of the state in which they provide ministry. Failure to comply with such statutes results in the same legal consequences that any person would encounter.

Ethical Accountability

As spiritual people providing spiritual ministry, chaplains feel accountability to a much higher source. They are accountable to God for their attitudes, motives, and actions. Ultimately, God wants the chaplain's heart, not a forced sense of accountability. As the Judeo-Christian Scriptures proclaim, "He has told you, O mortal, what is good; and what does the LORD require of you but to do justice, and to love kindness, and to walk humbly with your God?" (Micah 6:8, NRSV).

God requires the *right* response from chaplains as the people of God. That is, God compels chaplains to love mercy by having a compassionate heart that demonstrates godly action, and chaplains are to journey with God in obedience—not on the chaplain's path but on God's path.

Chaplains are professionals who voluntarily subscribe to a code of professional ethics. They consent to standards and protocols, asserting that they are also accountable to their own sense of morality and ethics. The chaplain is always at liberty to choose his or her own path of conscience with the implicit understanding and concession that they are also accountable to the law, their faith group, and the institution they serve.

CHAPTER 11

"Minefields" for the Chaplain

Privileged Communication, Confidentiality, & Privacy

Trust is a critical issue in the chaplain/client relationship. Spiritual and emotional healing can only take place where trust and transparency are present. When people are in distress, they are vulnerable and say things that they would ordinarily keep to themselves. Chaplains are often the guardians of very private or sacred information.

The distinctions of *privileged communication*, *confidentiality*, and *privacy* are very important. *Privileged communication* is a right established by law, *confidentiality* is an ethical concept applied by the chaplain, and *privacy* is a moral concept invoked by the client. These concepts are often discussed under the overarching umbrella of *confidential communication*.

Privileged Communication

Privileged communication is a legal term describing the prohibition of a client's confidence from being disclosed in a court of law without his or her consent. The right of privileged communication belongs to the client and is meant for the client's protection. While often perceived as being absolute, privileged communication *does* have its exemptions, even for the chaplain or clergy person. Forty-nine states have some form of privileged communications for clergy but also mandate reporting of child abuse. (Washington does not include clergy as mandated reporters.) The description of this privilege varies, and some states have specific exemptions. Many states specifically grant clergy-penitent privilege in pastoral communications but deny the privilege in cases of child abuse or neglect. Other states include clergy in a broad category of professional "other persons" who work with children. Because the laws vary from state to state, it is the responsibility of each chaplain to know the exceptions for his or her particular chaplain ministry setting.

Since the client's right of privileged communication is not inviolate, the same governing body that grants the privilege may revoke the privilege. Therefore, it is not a right that chaplains or clients should assume in all cases. These laws frequently change, requiring chaplains to remain vigilant regarding privilege changes. Chaplains should clarify the laws of the state or country in which they provide ministry and should engage legal counsel when uncertain about disclosure of information. Clergy-penitent privilege does not excuse a chaplain from being subpoenaed or appearing in court, but it does protect the chaplain from being forced to disclose privileged information during a deposition or court appearance. Usually, the appropriate attorney will make the objection for the chaplain.

Confidentiality

Confidentiality pertains to professional ethics whereby the chaplain assures the client of nondisclosure to the fullest extent allowed by law. Clients must be able to assume that their conversations will be kept confidential to ensure a spiritually and emotionally healing relationship with the chaplain. Some professionals, such as medical professionals, counselors, and attorneys, are legally required to maintain strict confidentiality. The law does *not* necessarily require a chaplain to maintain strict confidentiality, but in most cases, it *does* provide the opportunity for the chaplain to protect a client's confidential communication *if* the communication was conveyed to the chaplain acting in a professional capacity as a spiritual adviser (as opposed to talking to the chaplain as a golf partner, relative, or committee member). Generally, conversations in the presence of a third person are not considered confidential. (An exception would be an inmate who cannot speak to a chaplain without the presence of a guard.) Ultimately, the responsibility of keeping such a confidence belongs to the individual chaplain; therefore, the consequence for disclosure or nondisclosure also belongs to the chaplain.

> During a mentoring session, a colleague expressed concern over an issue of confidentiality and mandated reporting. "Chaplain, you realize that in Colorado clergy are mandated reporters? You could be criminally charged for withholding such information." "Yes, I am aware of the personal consequences *legally*, but it's a difficult position for me. I must choose between obeying the law or obeying my conscience to honor a child's hard-won trust in my confidentiality."

Confidentiality is also a moral concept supported in many faith traditions. The moral obligation of the chaplain is not absolute, however; thus, professional ethics determine when the confidentiality of the helping relationship might be broken. The chaplain may predetermine that a moral standard requires disclosure if the client is a threat to self or others. Or the chaplain may predetermine that in a medical emergency, personal information may need to be revealed to ensure the client's welfare or safety. Essentially, the chaplain must make a choice about breaking a promise or violating a covenant.

Chaplains should assure their clients that conversations are confidential, only if in fact they are. Some people fear that no conversations are confidential, so such assurances are necessary to build trust and confidence in clients to approach their chaplain for spiritual counseling. That is why, ethically, chaplains must inform the client when conversations are *not* absolutely confidential.

Privacy

The third term, *privacy*, relates to the concept that individuals have the right to choose for themselves the time and circumstances under which personal information might be disclosed to others. Privacy might be a moral concept that is supported in many faith traditions, but it is also a professional construct that is governed by several statutes, including the Privacy Act of 1974, the Health Insurance Portability and Accountability Act of 1996 (HIPAA), and the Americans with Disabilities Act of 1990 (ADA). These acts establish under which circumstances an individual's privacy may or may not be invaded, and they are intended as proactive measures against breaches of confidentiality. Chaplains are traditionally expected to be morally and ethically bound to honor these same privacy concepts.

Confidentiality & Privilege in the Workplace

Best practices in the workplace may include clear statements of policy regarding confidentiality and chaplain-client privilege, specifically stating exceptions based upon statutory requirements and institutional policy. The problematic issues are in the variables that arise—whether or not the institution is a private or publicly traded company, whether or not the institution deals with matters of national security, whether or not the institution's mission is law enforcement. Furthermore, clearly defining "imminent danger" to self, others, and national security may be ethical issues in and of themselves for the chaplain and the human resources department of the particular institution.

In the corporate environment, the Sarbanes-Oxley Act of 2002 addresses corporate governance and financial disclosure. However, in the world of the chaplain, there are presently few clearly defined rules for accountability in the area of privileged communication and disclosure.

Chaplains face more questions than answers. Without clearly stated policies, chaplains, their employers, and the endorsing religious organizations continue to struggle with the questions that arise in areas of personal choice, morals, values, or priorities. If chaplains do not initiate spiritual conversations but hear sensitive information during the *nonreligious* conversation, will the state consider the sensitive or incriminating information protected under the clergy/penitent privilege? When the chaplain is employed directly by the institution, where is the line between obligation to institutional policy and client confidentiality? What are the ethical issues surrounding confidentiality of withholding information about an employee with AIDS or other communicable diseases when they work in food processing plants or health-care facilities? What are the ethical issues surrounding illegal activity within the institution when the chaplain ministers to law enforcement personnel?

Most exceptions for client privilege deal with suicide, homicide, and child/elder abuse or neglect. But to whom are chaplains bound? Are they bound to their direct supervisors? Which ones—the supervisors in the institution that employs them or the supervisors in their ecclesiastical or religious body? Or are they bound only to the faith tradition they embrace?

For as solemnly as chaplains profess to maintain confidentiality, there are legal, ethical, and moral obligations that cause angst. Chaplains may eventually face an interesting dilemma: *When does the chaplain's high ethic of maintaining confidentiality make the chaplain a silent accomplice?* The questions are difficult to answer, and there are no clear-cut solutions to the problems that arise regarding privileged communication, confidentiality, and privacy. Chaplains will continue to struggle in the confluence of law, professional ethics, and morality.

Diagnosis & Assessment

Diagnoses and assessments are essential in the work of the chaplain. Accurate assessments are helpful as the chaplain plans ministry intervention, but a careless diagnosis and superficial assessment may create more harm than good. There is always a risk involved in assessing people's needs. Chaplains and clients are both vulnerable, and there is always the potential of inappropriate or damaging interventions.

The globalization of our nation and workplace has created cultural and religious diversity that in turn creates multiple needs and multiple expectations. The perception of needs varies among all clients based on cultural factors such as religion (or lack of religion), age, gender, ethnic heritage, economic status, physical disability, or previous trauma. In order to ease the tension of doing too much or doing too little, chaplains must have an intentional plan to assess and diagnose the client's needs.

> It was two o'clock in the morning when the phone rang, and the chaplain knew it would be an emergency. "I hope it's okay, Chaplain. Did I wake you? I had my first DOA [dead on arrival], and I can't quit thinking about it." With four simple words, the chaplain began her mental assessment: "Tell me about it. . . ."

Assessment provides valuable information for chaplains. It is foundational in planning ministry—prioritizing needs, triaging issues, setting goals for spiritual care. Ministry becomes goal-directed rather than symptom relieving. Assessments guide chaplains to deal with important matters first—to deal with the perceived issues as well as the real issues. When accurate information is gathered, there is a greater likelihood that an appropriate intervention will be considered and applied.

Chaplains are expected to do spiritual assessments, but if spirituality is about beliefs and values that give meaning to life and all that is held sacred, then chaplains must take a multidisciplinary approach to doing assessments. They must consider the spiritual, physical, emotional, relational, and cultural aspects of a person's being. As they complete this holistic assessment, they are better able to help people find hope and peace in their circumstances, to find God in their situation whether it be a crisis or a celebration.

Chaplains must complete assessments in order to prioritize needs, utilize appropriate and effective interventions, reduce vulnerability and risk, and set the stage for dialogue and communication between caregiver and client. Providing appropriate spiritual care is dependent on accurate diagnosis and assessments.

Personal Boundaries & Ethics

Chaplains are called to provide compassionate care for people. In doing so, they are constantly assessing and making decisions about a course of action. Objectivity and standard protocols are the *modus operandi* for chaplain interventions, but what happens in those gray areas where standards are not clearly stated or where personal preference could influence the decision? Respecting the boundaries of clients while honoring one's own boundaries may create tension for the chaplain. How does the chaplain deal with this tension, and by what standards does he or she function?

Boundaries are established for the mutual protection and accountability of chaplain and client. This is both a right and a responsibility. Setting boundaries must never be used as a form of manipulation. It is highly unethical and manipulative to arbitrarily set boundaries for each occasion or circumstance as a convenience or advantage for personal benefit. Boundaries must be set for the health and welfare of both chaplain and client. Setting and respecting boundaries is a way to empower those who are weak and to guard those who have the advantage. Boundaries define limits without having to say the word *no*.

Self-awareness

Setting appropriate boundaries begins with self-awareness. Chaplains must know what they are willing to do and what things are beyond their desire or willingness to do. Reflection and meditation may help clarify the limits for chaplains. Ask yourself, "As a Christian, am I willing to pray without saying, 'In Jesus' name . . .'?" "As a Muslim, am I willing to administer the bread and cup when asked?" "As a Jew, am I willing to conduct interfaith worship (as differentiated from multifaith worship) on Saturdays?" Or even more practically, "Am I willing to be on-call 24 hours a day, 365 days a year?" Chaplains must be aware of those things that empower them and those activities that they would rather avoid—perhaps out of conscience, fear, inability, lack of experience, or disinterest.

The Hebrew scriptures say, "Above all else, guard your heart, for it is the wellspring of life" (Proverbs 4:23). Self-awareness means knowing what you want and don't want, knowing what you are willing to do or not do, knowing what you can do or cannot do, knowing your strengths and weaknesses, and knowing what energizes and empowers you or what depletes you. Self-awareness means being honest with yourself.

Safety

Some criteria chaplains may use to determine appropriate boundaries may include the basic issues of *safety, legality, morality,* and *ethics*. Some chaplain settings create a special awareness of safety issues. Law enforcement chaplains deal with the possibility of dangerous suspected criminals, shootings, or high-speed vehicle chases. Fire chaplains deal with burning buildings, electrical and water hazards, or uncontrollable wildfires. Hospital chaplains deal with communicable diseases, radiation exposure, or hostile family members. Sports chaplains deal with accidents, avalanches, and stampedes. Industrial chaplains deal with explosions, toxic waste, or workplace violence. Correctional chaplains deal with fights, murders, and escapes. Crisis intervention chaplains deal with unpredictable natural disasters, food contamination, and health hazards. Military chaplains deal with war, bombings, and riots. In every setting, chaplains deal with issues that threaten or compromise their safety. Each chaplain must make intentional decisions about appropriate safety boundaries. Ask yourself, "What am I willing to do? Where am I willing to go? Who am I willing to see?"

Legality

Most chaplains would say, "I wouldn't intentionally break the law." But there are times when chaplains may need to clarify their own boundaries regarding what is legal and what is *right*. Chaplains are not exempt from the law. Setting boundaries means knowing the conditions under which one is willing to suffer the consequences of breaking the law. Breaking the law definitely has consequences. Shielding the criminal, nondisclosure, violating the right to free exercise of religion—these are decisions that have serious consequences. Chaplains must know the statutes that affect their ministry and set appropriate boundaries against those individuals who would manipulate or coerce them into illegal activity.

Morality

There are moral principles that govern the ministry of a chaplain. These principles are usually based on personal values and principles. They often reflect the chaplain's faith and tenets of his or her religious belief. As such, the chaplain's faith group may establish boundaries that the chaplain must accept or reject. Again, this requires self-awareness and the ability to set appropriate boundaries. The chaplain may say, "My church does not allow me to baptize people outside my faith tradition, but I will contact a minister who will be pleased to baptize your baby." Morals are personally held beliefs; therefore, they may clash with the beliefs of clients whose culture or religion is different or even abhorrent to the chaplain. Setting boundaries is not about being right. It is about doing what one believes is morally acceptable and demonstrating grace to those whose values and principles differ.

Ethics

The chaplain functions at the invitation of an institution (e.g., NASCAR, the US Army, or South County Jail) and is governed by certain accepted professional standards. These are the ethical standards for which chaplains also establish boundaries. Within these institutions or similar organizations, chaplains and administrators have established professional standards for the ministry actions of chaplains. Setting appropriate boundaries means knowing what actions are acceptable and establishing personal limits in light of those standards. For example, some institutions may consider it an ethics violation if a chaplain dates an employee, or if a chaplain accepts expensive gifts from a patient, or if a chaplain provides legal advice for an inmate, or if a chaplain carries a sidearm. Chaplains must be willing to accept the ethical standards of the institution—or set their own boundaries and be willing to accept the consequences as administered by the institution.

When chaplains set boundaries, simple and direct language is most effective. Since boundaries are personal, there is no need to explain or defend one's position. Fear of rejection and guilt sabotage the boundaries that a chaplain establishes. When boundaries are set with right intentions and respect for others, they set healthy limits to action, relationships, and self-care for the chaplain. Healthy boundaries allow the chaplain and client to set empowering standards for behavior and interpersonal relationships.

A chaplain must always be guarded about boundary violations—his or her own and those of the client. The most violated boundaries are physical and emotional. On the chaplain's part, standing too close to a person without that person's permission is an infringement of his or her personal space. Touching people without permission—no matter how innocent—is unethical and inappropriate. People have the right to refuse handshakes, hugs, and hand-holding. Some cultures even forbid it. Eavesdropping on conversations, searching through or handling other people's personal property without permission, and otherwise violating a person's right to privacy are other ways physical boundaries are trespassed.

Perhaps the most painful boundary violations are those that affect people emotionally. While no chaplain would yell or scream at a client—which is abusive at its very core—breaking commitments, telling people they should or should not do something, or assuming a patronizing attitude could be equally abusive. A memory for names and details, cultural sensitivity, honesty, commitment, and extending grace are qualities that show respect for emotional boundaries.

Chaplain Misconduct

What causes misconduct among chaplains? Could it be the wrong attitude? Chaplains are not exempt from questionable behavior. They often struggle to find the black and white as they muddle through the gray. Chaplains who believe they are invulnerable are naïve and unrealistic about their abilities and perhaps the motives of others. Chaplain misconduct is a betrayal of sacred trust.

Chaplains live in the tension of setting appropriate personal and professional boundaries while respecting the boundaries of others. With a clear understanding of their own faith, values, and beliefs, chaplains make the difficult decisions that exist in the gray areas of ministry. Chaplains each must consider safety, legality, morality, and ethics as they set and maintain boundaries.

CHAPTER 12

Health and Empowerment for the Chaplain

The work of the chaplain provides great rewards and fulfillment. The ministry includes opportunities to perform religious tasks, spiritual care, advocacy, and spiritual healing in addition to many other services specific to the particular setting in which the chaplain works. No matter the setting, however, the demands of spiritual care ministry may prove taxing on the chaplain. Intentionally choosing to walk alongside and share the burdens of people in need results in physical, emotional, and spiritual fatigue for the caregiver.

Institutions

The institutions that employ chaplains often have programs for maintaining employee health through the human resources department or employee assistance programs. The irony is that chaplaincy is often considered a form of employee assistance. Through company self-help groups and company referrals, the chaplain, too, may receive professional help when necessary. Financial stress, substance abuse, divorce—these are real problems for real people. The chaplain is not immune to the same issues and crises that all people face. Employee assistance counselors may provide referrals, educational materials, and other resources to keep the chaplain healthy. After all, healthy chaplains are an asset to the institution.

Professional Organizations

Professional organizations, too, recognize chaplain vulnerability and provide resources and networking opportunities for chaplains. The Association of Professional Chaplains (APC) and other chaplain organizations present annual conferences with myriad workshops and seminars to inform and encourage chaplains in their professional and personal lives. These chaplain organizations usually have state organizations that also host monthly or quarterly in-service trainings and meetings for peer support. The APC requires board certified chaplains to maintain their credentials by participating in a minimum number of hours of conferences, support groups, and other activities each year. The International Conference of Police Chaplains and the Association of Fire Chaplains have conducted annual conferences for many years. The Yale Center for Faith and Culture in joint efforts with Tyson Foods, Inc., have also sponsored similar conferences with an emphasis on workplace chaplaincy.

Self-care

Ultimately, health and empowerment for the chaplain begins with self-care. Chaplains must initiate good, lifelong habits of self-care. These habits may include eating a well-balanced diet, participating in regular physical exercise, maintaining significant relationships, getting adequate rest and sleep, and having an active prayer and devotional life, in addition to the various requirements of a chaplain's institution or ecclesiastical body. Effective self-care involves preventive maintenance as well as asking for help when personal resources are inadequate to maintain physical, emotional, and spiritual health.

On a very practical level, preventative maintenance includes reducing refined sugars, caffeine, fats, alcohol, salt, and cholesterol; increasing cardiovascular exercise; getting six to eight hours of sleep each night; being an active participant in a faith community; maintaining healthy relationships with loved ones and associates by balancing work and personal life; and making time for recreation, hobbies, vacations, or sabbaticals.

The work of the chaplain may be very stressful, and burnout is the most obvious reaction to long-term stress. Burnout is the emotional, mental, and physical exhaustion that occurs when several events in succession or a combination of other stressors impose a high degree of stress on an individual. There are several contributing factors in chaplain burnout. These may include such issues as professional isolation, ambiguous successes, maintaining an unrealistic pace, "Messiah Complex," and human finitude. Chaplains who are experiencing burnout may feel isolation, depression, apathy, or pessimism. They may feel indifferent or even hopeless. Symptoms include physical exhaustion, behavioral irritability, or emotional negativity. Chaplains experiencing these feelings may be entering the beginning stages of a more complex problem—compassion fatigue.

Compassion Fatigue

Compassion fatigue is a secondary form of post-traumatic stress that only affects caregivers, including chaplains. It may occur when a chaplain vicariously experiences a trauma event by providing spiritual care to a client who was the actual person experiencing the traumatic event—by listening to the story of the event or experiencing the reactions to the trauma through empathetic contact with the client. Vulnerability caused by depleted resources—burnout—may prevent chaplains from preserving a critical distance between themselves and the event. It is the costly result of inadequate self-care and constant caregiving to clients who are suffering from many kinds of crises and traumatic life events.

One of the most profound issues of chaplain stress or burnout is the inevitable *change* it causes in the chaplain's life and ministry. Some physical changes such as anxiety or high blood pressure are very temporary, and chaplains manage to return to full health and function within a normal time frame. However, when chaplains are subjected to long-term stress and the resulting reactions of mental and physical exhaustion, they often experience changes in their values and beliefs. That which was held as *sacred* has been violated. Perspectives have changed. Chaplains may experience doubt and uncertainty regarding their calling, the value of their ministry, or even their faith.

> In the aftermath of Hurricane Rita, for some chaplains who were also clergy persons with congregational responsibilities, four months of ministry to victims and congregants was too much. They were physically exhausted, emotionally depleted, and weary of government promises and excuses. They questioned their calling as clergy and reconsidered social ministry.

Health and empowerment for the chaplain begin with intentional preventative self-care and are maintained by institutional, professional, and peer support. If you are a chaplain in crisis, STOP. Get help. You must take care of yourself before you can help others. The ministry of compassion and caring must come from the overflow of God's compassion and caring in your life. If life is full of questions, your resources are depleted, and you are facing a crisis of belief, take what many in the Christian tradition call an "Emmaus walk" (see Luke 24:13-22). Allow the spirit of God to walk along with you—to answer questions, to clarify options, and to fellowship with you. When you feel connected once more to the presence of God, you will be restored and empowered to do the work of the chaplain.

"Therefore Go . . . "

The work of the chaplain begins with intentional preparation for spiritual care ministry—seminary education, specific training in counseling and leadership, and integration of life experiences with personal reflection to gain an appreciation for the perspectives of people very different than oneself. With institutional awareness and a desire to walk with people through all circumstances of life, the chaplain takes God's presence to the world in battlefields, surgical waiting rooms, manufacturing plants, think tanks, fire houses, dormitory lobbies, homeless shelters, racetracks, casinos, evacuation centers, or emergency disaster mortuaries.

For the Christian chaplain, this ministry is part of fulfilling the Great Commission, proclaimed by Jesus on the mountain before he ascended again into heaven:

> "Therefore go and make disciples of all nations, baptizing them in the name of the Father and of the Son and of the Holy Spirit, and teaching them to obey everything I have commanded you. And surely I am with you always, to the very end of the age." (Matthew 28:18-20)

The Christian chaplain is committed to proclaim God's love to a world that may never step through the doors of a church; therefore, the chaplain steps through the doors of the church into the world. Taking the initiative to meet people in their pain and suffering requires courage and compassion. The chaplain intentionally chooses to enter into the lives of people, accompanying them on a journey that may include hardship as well as joy.

As a minister in an environment of differing cultures, interests, and religions, the chaplain is a religious pluralist, seeking ways to allow all people to express their faith or lack of faith in meaningful ways, being inclusive without compromising his or her own faith. Without proselytizing, the Christian chaplain evangelizes the world through his or her own character, integrity, compassion, and witness. As chaplains minister to the spiritual needs of people, they engage in spiritual conversations that often lead to opportunities to share their personal faith and religious beliefs.

When direct evangelistic conversations don't materialize, Christian chaplains do "pre-evangelism"—laying the foundation for future opportunities to share the gospel. They demonstrate true compassion, genuine interest in the lives of their clients, and *agape* love for all people. In the words of St. Francis of Assisi, chaplains must "preach the gospel at all times and when necessary use words."

Chaplains minister in the tension of seeking to find balance—between serving God, serving people, and serving the institution that employs them; between their accountability to the ecclesiastical body that endorses them and to the institution that retains them; between being a spiritual caregiver and a religious provider; between being inclusive of all faith traditions and not compromising their own beliefs; between providing meaningful spiritual care and knowing when to refer to a specialist. Spiritual maturity, a servant heart, and humility are essential attitudes for the successful chaplain.

It is our hope that any who seeks the work of the chaplain will be blessed by any insights found in these pages. May you fulfill God's calling upon your life and bring the kingdom of God ever nearer to the people of God.

APPENDIX A

Preparing for the Work of the Chaplain

Every vocation requires both general and specific training and preparation. So it is with the work of the chaplain. Chaplain work is *spiritual* work—including a clear vocational calling and theological training. Chaplain work is *clinical* work—including supervised clinical training, credentialing, and continuing education. Chaplain work is *vocational* work—including institutional awareness, specialized education, and training. Successful and rewarding chaplain ministry begins with an awareness of necessary preparations for initiating ministry as a chaplain.

Vocational Calling

The work of the chaplain begins with God's call to ministry. Every person experiences God's call in one way or another. It may be the call to saving faith or the call to faithful discipleship. A call to chaplain ministry, however, is a unique call, which is preceded by a clear call to vocational service in spiritual care.

How does one know he or she has been "called" to chaplain ministry? Some have heard the audible voice of God, and others have had a compelling vision from God. Like the Jewish prophet Isaiah, they encountered God and the encounter caused a significant response—deepening faith, voicing commitment, or strengthening service: "Here I am. Send me" (Isaiah 6:8). Others have approached chaplain ministry with less certainty because they did not have such a dramatic experience. Perhaps they have felt God's unrelenting tugging and pulling on their heart or in their spirit. Maybe they have spent sleepless nights struggling with God, knowing that there was an urgent reason to consider new possibilities for ministry. Others have been affirmed by pastors, friends, and family. Everyone began with a step of faith, because God didn't send an e-mail, fax, or certified letter. Whether the call was clear and concise or whether the call seemed ambiguous and tentative, there was a defining moment when each chaplain intentionally chose to follow the Master's will—as a servant. At such a moment, came fulfillment in obeying *the call.*

Discerning God's will for a life is often a lifelong quest. But trust God to use every experience in your spiritual journey. Many candidates will verify the call to chaplain ministry through diagnostic inventories and assessments. Some will participate in interviews or reviews by peers, local faith communities, or larger ecclesiastical bodies. Others will follow the spirit of God through meditation, study of scripture, prayer, and circumstance. But ultimately, people seem *to know* that God has called them to chaplain ministry when they have a passion to "carry each other's burdens" (Galatians 6:2), to provide ministry to "the least of these" (Matthew 25:40), and to "go" (Matthew 28:19).

Don't be in a hurry. Relationships take time. God wants to build a lasting relationship with those who are called to chaplain ministry. He will provide the training and education at the right time. He will provide the right opportunities at the right time. He will provide the encouragement and nurture all the time. Graciously, God also provides the *gifting* and the aptitudes at the right time, too. God asks the chaplain to have the right attitude and the patience to wait until the fullness of God's own time.

Why would anyone want a job that often requires 24-hour on-call status, stepping into uncomfortable and sometimes dangerous settings, walking with hurt and despairing people through pain and suffering, or experiencing only ambiguous successes? Why would anyone want a job that might pay too little, expect too much, or make unrealistic demands? Only you can answer these questions. Has God called *you* to be a chaplain?

Theological Training

Chaplains are first and foremost fully trained clergy representing their own faith group in a chaplaincy setting. Since they typically minister in a pluralistic setting, it is imperative that they are confident about what they believe as a chaplain representing that faith group, or they are likely to become one who believes anything and everything they encounter. That is one major reason for acquiring a theological education. Another reason is that theological education usually qualifies a chaplain to become an ordained clergy person, able to perform the sacraments or ordinances as well as the religious services and roles required of one's faith group.

Presently the Department of Defense allows a chaplain to apply for a federal chaplaincy position with 72 semester hours of study, which is usually equal to a Master of Arts (MA), plus a few electives. The MA must consist of no less than 36 hours in theological/biblical studies from a seminary accredited through the Association of Theological Schools (ATS). Many judicatories and some chaplaincy positions may not be satisfied with an MA degree since an MA degree is not as intense or complete as a full Master of Divinity (MDiv), which consists of 90-plus semester hours of theological study. However, as long as the minimal educational requirements are met, one could become a chaplain with a Master of Arts (MA) and additional electives to equal 72 semester hours rather than an MDiv.

Even if some chaplaincy positions are available to those with an MA, if there are two applicants for the position who are equal in every other way but one has an MDiv and the other an MA, the MDiv holder will usually have the advantage in the hiring process. The applicant with an MA rather than an MDiv may deem it necessary to return to a seminary to "upgrade" that degree to an MDiv. Prospective chaplains should check with their faith group endorser and desired employer for the preferred theological degree prior to pursuing that education.

Clinical Training

Most forms of chaplaincy require practical clinical training prior to employment. Part of this requirement is a minimum of two years of ministerial experience, usually postseminary. This is so that the chaplain is able to fully represent their faith group as a competent clergyperson. Many forms of chaplaincy (hospital, hospice, elder care, etc.) as well as some professional chaplaincy organizations such as the Association of Professional Chaplains (APC) require the successful completion of a minimum of one to four units of Clinical Pastoral Education (CPE). CPE is an educational delivery system based on an action-reflection-evaluation educational field model that helps students develop their spiritual formation, competence, and reflection skills.

Other forms of chaplaincy (crisis and disaster, military, police, fire, hospital, etc.) require chaplains to have training in Critical Incident Stress Management. This training prepares chaplains for spiritual care to the first responders (police, firefighters, EMTs) on the scene of mass casualty disasters. Self-aid and buddy-care first-aid training are useful for all forms of chaplaincy since chaplains are often involved in emergency and disaster work. Of course, no one can be in ministry without being called on to be a counselor, so the wise chaplain will want to be trained in crisis counseling and brief counseling skills for the many short-term chaplaincy encounters.

Religious Requirements

The religious endorsing body has the prerogative to define the requirements for ordination and endorsement within its faith group. (Some faith traditions do not ordain, but commission, accredit, or certify their chaplains—especially in the case of female candidates.) Some faith groups demand many years of graduate and postgraduate requirements plus the practical steps to ordination and endorsement, while others have minimal expectations and requirements for their chaplains. Most Christian denominations define "two years of ministerial experience" quite narrowly—only local senior pastoral experience after earning the MDiv. Other faith groups allow for many differing forms of ministerial experience, and some count paid or even volunteer work while in seminary as part or all of that pastoral experience. Usually the more hierarchical the religious group, the more involved and lengthy is the process. A prudent prospective chaplain should first determine which endorsing body he or she wishes to represent and with which to be affiliated, and then ascertain that body's current endorsement criteria for the chaplaincy.

Credentials

Credentials often serve as an important way for chaplains to "prove" their professionalism to institutional employers and constituents. Most forms of chaplaincy require the chaplain to be an ordained and endorsed clergyperson from a nationally recognized faith group and possessor of an MDiv degree from an ATS accredited seminary. Hospital chaplains and a few other chaplains are further required to have completed a minimum of four CPE units. Those same four units are a part of the requirement to become a Board Certified Chaplain with the APC.

Memberships in one or more professional organizations are also a form of professional credentialing. Chaplains often seek membership in broad-based chaplain organizations such as the APC or the Association of Clinical Pastoral Education, or in organizations specific to their form of chaplaincy, such as one for police, business, prison, hospice or military chaplains, etc. Chaplains are often members of one or more professional counseling organizations as well, such as the American Association of Pastoral Counselors or the American Association of Christian Counselors.

Some chaplaincies require that their chaplains hold credentials (or "insider status") from the institution in which they serve. For instance, military chaplains must also be commissioned military officers. Police and fire chaplains are often fully licensed and credentialed police officers and firefighters prior to being accepted as chaplains. Campus chaplains often are expected to be able to hold faculty status, and many times sports chaplains were involved in some way with the sport prior to being accepted as a chaplain.

Institutional Awareness

Ministry in an institution requires a special understanding and awareness of that particular institution. Government agencies (e.g., US military, FBI, Federal Bureau of Corrections, Veteran's Administration hospitals) are complicated and have many bureaucratic idiosyncrasies that may cause chaplains some anxiety. Corporate, industry, or other businesses also have regulations, policies, and procedures that have governmental oversight or industry monitoring through statutes and standards. Law enforcement and other first responder institutions have safety protocols, legal implications, unspoken rules, and invisible barriers that chaplains face. In each chaplain ministry setting, there are unique issues and foci that require conscious chaplain awareness.

When chaplains enter the institutional culture without having ever been a part of that culture, they are faced with the challenge of building trust and credibility—by the institution and the employees. The school district worries about chaplains meeting with students, and the students wonder if they can trust a chaplain. The county jail is concerned about the chaplain's motives, and the inmates are convinced the chaplain is working for "the man." A consistent presence and interest in the "business," coupled with intentional observation and study of the culture and distinctive traits of the institution assist the chaplain in understanding the basics of the institution.

Chaplains must know the business—what is its goal, how is it accomplished, what makes it successful, what hinders it, who are the employees, who are the customers, what makes it valuable? This *intellectual* understanding may be accomplished by reading company reports, researching on the Internet, or talking to the public relations officer. Accomplishing the *emotional* understanding of the institutional culture will require building relationships with the people within the institution.

> The company was led by an executive team of predominantly white, Anglo, Christian, highly successful men. As part of the community involvement initiative, the company decided on a food drive to benefit the community food pantry. The reasons for company involvement seemed obvious—help the hungry. But employee response seemed to be mostly that of disinterest. What was the problem? After considering the culture represented by the executive team in contrast with the culture represented by the employees, it was discovered that white, Anglo Christians respond to hunger needs a little bit differently than the general Asian culture represented by the employees. For the Asian employees, collecting food was a "nice" thing to do, but *families* "should" take care of their own. Employees were more inclined to participate in community involvement if the projects were for things their families did not typically deal with individually.

For chaplains, part of knowing the business they are engaged in is "knowing the customer." The "customer" is both the institution and the individuals within the institution. Thus, the chaplain ministers *to* the institution and ministers *within* the institution. Knowing the business and knowing the people who are engaged in the business result in effective ministry within the institutional culture. Institutional awareness is intentional preparation for the work of the chaplain.

Finding and Keeping a Position as a Chaplain

Until recently, chaplain positions have not been well advertised outside the realm of the military and health-care. Consequently, people seeking positions as professional (paid) chaplains must be aggressive and creative in their search. But the basics for finding a job remain the same. Finding and keeping a position as a chaplain involve preparation, presentation, and performance.

Chaplains must first search for positions that "fit." They must find positions that meet their specific call, mission, and gifting. Job markets, companies, and employers must be researched and broadly considered. The usual research involves utilizing public or seminary libraries and referrals from clergy, colleagues, family, or friends. The Internet has also made finding chaplain jobs in many settings much easier than it has been in the past. You may read job listings, post a résumé, dialogue with potential employers, and even begin the application process online.

Chaplains must also present themselves well. Applications and résumés must be flawlessly written. Interviews must be professional conversations that reflect competence, passion, honesty, compatibility, and a cooperative attitude.

After securing the position as a chaplain, no measure of education or experience will replace the consistent demonstration of godly character, professional competence, a compassionate heart, and a sincere desire to be a lifelong learner. Chaplains often influence the longevity of their own professional relationship with an institution by maintaining their value in the institution. That is, chaplains who provide unique services to the institution and who demonstrate that their services are a necessary part of institutional functioning, health, and profitability will be considered an *essential* component of the institution.

Professional and Vocational Organizations

Chaplains gain much insight about finding and keeping positions through professional and vocational organizations. Chaplain organizations such as the Association of Professional Chaplains (APC) or the National Association of Catholic Chaplains (NACC) provide information on job and training opportunities, networking possibilities, discussion forums, and resources for such things as program development, sample documents (e.g., job descriptions, institutional policies), and templates for worship services, prayers, and litanies.

Other professional and vocational organizations provide similar resources. Clinical or counseling organizations are often places where chaplains find positions. Some of these organizations may include the American Association of Pastoral Counselors (AAPC), the Association for Clinical Pastoral Education (ACPE), the National Conference on Ministry to the Armed Forces (NCMAF), and the College of Pastoral Supervision and Psychotherapy (CPSP). Others are listed in Appendix C.

Specific Institutions

An institution seeking a chaplain presents its specialized requirements as part of the job description. However, if a chaplain is presenting himself or herself *to* an institution as a possibility for hire, there are a few preliminaries that the chaplain must consider.

Gaining access to the institution—the executive who does the hiring—requires that the potential chaplain first demonstrate value to the organization. The chaplain could establish a network inside the company (not necessarily at the executive level) and a network outside the company at places where company or institutional employees and executives make themselves visible. This could include participation in service organizations, the United Way, or the Little League. Chaplains may also make themselves available through the direct approach during corporate crisis or a time of personal crisis. Reading about an institutional accident or the death of an employee may give the potential chaplain an opportunity to provide meaningful spiritual care while allowing the institution to experience the potential of a professional chaplain.

Finding and keeping a position as a chaplain also entails being informed about the business, the institutional environment, or the industry culture. It involves being informed about institutional needs and implementing plans to meet those needs. Appendix A discusses institutional awareness as a necessary component for chaplain ministry *preparation*, but the changing climate of institutions also makes institutional awareness a necessary component of *keeping* a chaplain position.

Continuing Education

Many employers and employees have discovered that continuing education is more than an investment in a chaplain's career. It also increases productivity and keeps the chaplain competitive in the marketplace. From the chaplain's perspective, it provides training and education that keeps the chaplain credible with the institution and helps the chaplain sharpen skills to better minister to the employees.

Most professions require continuing education as a means to maintain chaplain competence and relevance in a changing world. The APC requires its board-certified chaplains to participate in a minimum of 50 hours of continuing education each year to maintain certification. Breadth of continuing education is equally important. Board-certified chaplains must experience continuing education in at least three different categories, including teaching and supervising; workshops, conference, seminars, or symposia; papers, publications, or books written; self-instruction; formal academic courses; or personal growth and therapy. There are other categories of continuing education as well. The objective of continuing education certainly may be described as stressing the importance of professional and personal growth to maintain, elevate, and anticipate higher qualifications; to improve ministry interventions; and to achieve more satisfaction in pastoral work.

Many institutions require continuing education for their chaplains. This may take the form of institutional in-service training, classes, or seminars. Or it could take the form of formal or academic training through recognized agencies for certification or credentialing. Just as law enforcement officers must be recertified in the use of handguns or other tactical weapons, chaplains must be recertified in crisis intervention, CPR, and suicide prevention skills. Institutions are in the business of excelling within their industry, and requiring chaplain competence is another way to maintain their competitive edge.

Whether the continuing education is a requirement within the profession or a requirement to keep the job, chaplains are reminded that they serve God even as they serve God's people. The Christian scriptures exhort, "Whatever your task, put yourselves into it, as done for the Lord and not for your masters" (Colossians 3:23, NRSV).

The journey of lifelong learning is a journey of discovery, insight, and enrichment. Continuing education helps the chaplain intentionally nurture quality spiritual care, and it is a means to finding and keeping a position as a chaplain.

Entrepreneurial Approach

The chaplain who cannot find a position that meets his or her needs may by necessity have to create a position—taking the entrepreneurial approach to chaplain ministry. The chaplain establishes and finances a new enterprise—a ministry—to find the balance between meeting his or her financial needs and meeting real ministry needs.

The chaplain begins by identifying an institution where he or she desires to provide chaplain ministry and then develops a business plan and a financial plan. The business plan answers all the initial questions a prospective employer/institution might have, for example:

1. What is the vision or what is it that the chaplain will do?
2. What is the market or to whom will the chaplain provide ministry?
3. How will the chaplain capture the market—ensuring the desirability of the chaplain services?
4. What is the value proposition—or from the institution's perspective, "What's in it for me?"
5. How will the plan be implemented?
6. How will the chaplain of a particular faith background minister to people who practice a different religion—or no religion at all?
7. What will be the measure of success or effectiveness?
8. What will be the milestones for measuring the success?

The chaplain must also develop a financial plan based on many assumptions—including the assumption that the institution will "buy" the idea. Financial plans are usually three-year projections detailing the initial investment, the cost for implementation, and the capital investment—all against the number of clients or persons being served by chaplain ministry. When the chaplain is prepared with the business and financial plans, he or she should approach the highest decision maker in the institution with the new enterprise.

Professional chaplaincy is often considered a new element of traditional employee assistance programs. As such, many companies will not consider a full-time chaplain, but may consider a 4-hour-a-week chaplain or an 8-hour-a-week chaplain. This means entrepreneurial chaplains must find multiple settings and produce multiple business plans that are specific to each institution. In any given week, such a chaplain may provide ministry for as many as ten different institutions or for multiple locations of several institutions. Alternatively, some chaplains may need to hold a paying job or raise their own financial support (as many missionaries do) while developing an entrepreneurial chaplain position. Some "umbrella" chaplaincy organization (e.g., Motor Racing Outreach or other sports, industrial, or prison organizations) administer this financial support for the chaplain. Other chaplains create a 501(c)3 nonprofit chaplaincy organization from which to minister.

The entrepreneurial approach to creating a chaplain ministry often requires significant amounts of energy, creative thinking, and persistence. When chaplains respond to God's call upon their lives, they are assured that God will enable them to accomplish all that is necessary and right (see Hebrews 13:21).

Resources for Chaplain Ministry

Prominent Professional Organizations

This list offers a substantial starting place for chaplains and prospective chaplains interested in exploring affiliation or membership with larger chaplaincy groups. It is by no means an exhaustive list.

American Association of Christian Counselors (AACC)
PO Box 739
Forest, VA 24551
(800) 526-8673
(434) 525-9480 FAX
www.AACC.net

American Association of Pastoral Counselors (AAPC)
9504 A Lee Hwy
Fairfax, VA 22031
(703) 385-6967
(703) 352-7725 FAX
www.aapc.org

American Correctional Chaplains Association (ACCA)
Box 422
East Lyme, CT 06333
(860) 691-6549
(860) 739-9375 FAX
www.correctionalchaplains.org

Association for Clinical Pastoral Education (ACPE)
1549 Clairmont Rd, Ste 103
Decatur, GA 30033-4635
(404) 320-1472
(404) 320-0849 FAX
www.acpe.edu

Association of Professional Chaplains (APC)
1701 E. Woodfield Rd, Ste 760
Schaumburg, IL 60173-5109
(847) 240-1014
(847) 240-1015 FAX
www.professionalchaplains.org

Canadian Association for Pastoral
Practice & Education (CAPPE)
7960 St. Margaret's Bay Rd
Ingramport, NS B3Z 3Z7
CANADA
(866) 442-2773
(902) 820-3087 FAX
www.cappe.org

College of Pastoral Supervision
& Psychotherapy (CPSP)
PO Box 162
432 W. 47th St, 2W
Times Square Station
New York, NY 10108
(212) 246-6410
(212) 305-5666 FAX
www.cpsp.org

Council on Ministries in Specialized
Settings (COMISS)
PO Box 2409
Poquoson, VA 23662
(757) 728-3180
(707) 929-7388 FAX
www.comissnetwork.org

International Conference of
Police Chaplains (ICPC)
PO Box 5590
Destin, FL 32540-5590
(850) 654-9736
(850) 654-9742 FAX
icpc@icpc.gccoxmail.com

National Association of Catholic
Chaplains (NACC)
PO Box 070473
Milwaukee, WI 53207-0473
(414) 483-4898
(414) 483-6712 FAX
www.nacc.org

National Association of Jewish Chaplains
(NAJC)
901 Route 10
Whippany, NJ 07981-1156
(973) 929-3168
(973) 736-9193 FAX
www.najc.org

National Conference on Ministry to the
Armed Forces (NCMAF)
7708 Griffin Pond Ct
Springfield, VA 22153
(703) 455-7908
(703) 455-7948 FAX
www.ncmaf.org

National Institute of Business &
Industrial Chaplaincy (NIBIC)
1770 St. James Place, Ste 550
Houston, TX 77056
(713) 266-2456
(713) 266-0845 FAX
www.nibic.com

New York Board of Rabbis (NYBR)
Chaplaincy Commission
136 E. 39th St, 4th Floor
New York, NY 10016-0914
(212) 983-3521
(212) 983-3531 FAX
www.nybr.org

Religious Endorsing Bodies

This list represents just a sampling of more than 230 religious endorsing bodies. For additional organizations and contact information, contact:

The National Conference on Ministry to the Armed Forces (NCMAF)
& Endorsers Conference for Veterans Affairs Chaplaincy
4141 N Henderson Rd, Ste 13 / Arlington, VA 22203
(703) 455-7908 / (703) 276-7948 FAX
E-mail: jack@ncmaf.org or maureen@ncmaf.org

Alliance of Baptists
www.allianceofbaptists.org

American Baptist Chaplaincy & Pastoral Counseling Services
www.abc-cpcs.org

Apostolic Catholic Orthodox Church
www.apostoliccatholic.org

Assemblies of God, General Council of
www.chaplaincy.ag.org

Baptist General Convention of Texas
www.bgct.org/TexasBaptists

Christian Church (Disciples of Christ)
www.disciples.org
dthompson@dhm.disciples.org

Christian Church of North America Christ Fellowship Church
www.spirit-filled.org

Christian Reformed Church in North America
www.crcna.org/chaplaincy

Church of Christ
chaplainfcoc@worldnet.att.net

Church of God (Anderson, Indiana)
www.chog.org

Churches of God, General Conference
Paparson@aol.com

Church of Jesus Christ of Latter-day Saints (LDS)
clawsonfw@ldschurch.org

Church of the Nazarene
djennings@nazarene.org

Coalition of Spirit-Filled Churches (CSC)
Also: International Ministerial Fellowship, Christian Church of North America, Christ's Church Fellowship
www.spirit-filled.org

Conservative Baptist Association of America (CBA)
www.cbcchaplains.net

Cooperative Baptist Fellowship
www.cbfnet.org

Episcopal Church Endorsement Office of the Bishop of Chaplains
www.ecusa-chaplain.org

Evangelical Church Alliance (ECA)
www.ecainternational.org

The Evangelical Covenant Church
www.covchurch.org/ministry

Evangelical Free Church of America
www.efca.org/chaplains

Evangelical Lutheran Church of America (ELCA)
www.elca.org/chaplains

The Full Gospel Churches
Also: The Association of Vineyard Churches
www.chaplaincyfullgospel.org

Islamic Society of North America
www.siss.edu

Lutheran Church–Missouri Synod
www.lcms.org/spm

National Association of Catholic Chaplains
www.nacc.org

National Association of Evangelicals (NAE)
www.nae.net

National Baptist Convention of America, Inc.
jwdaile@aol.com

National Baptist Convention USA, Inc.
drcthomas1@cs.com

National Jewish Welfare Board/Jewish Chaplains Council
Also: General Conference of American Rabbis (JWB), Rabbinical Assembly, Conservative (JWB), Rabbinical Council of America (Orthodox) (JWB)
www.jcca.org

Pentecostal Church of God, Inc.
lmboyles@aol.com

Presbyterian Council for Chaplains & Military Personnel (PC)
Also: Presbyterian Church (USA) The Associate Reformed Presbyterian Church, The Cumberland Presbyterian Church, The Cumberland Presbyterian Church in America
www.erols.com/pccmp and www.pcusa.org

Presbyterian & Reformed Joint Commission on Chaplains and Military Personnel (PRJC)
Also: Korean-American Presbyterian Church, Korean Presbyterian Church in America, The Orthodox Presbyterian Church, The Presbyterian Church in America (PCA), Reformed Presbyterian Church of North America
www.pcanet.org

Progressive National Baptist Convention, Inc.
BobnJackie@juno.com

Reformed Church in America (RCA)
www.rca.org

Regular Baptist Churches, General Association of
www.garbc.org

Roman Catholic Church
jroque@milarch.org

Seventh-day Adventists US, General Conference of
www.adventischaplains.org

Southern Baptist Convention North American Mission Board
www.namb.net/chaplain

United Church of Christ
www.ucc.org

United Methodist Church General Board of Higher Education and Ministry
www.gbhem.org/chaplains

United Pentecostal Church International
www.upci.org or www.ugst.org

World Council of Independent Christian Churches
www.wcicc.org

Recommended Reading

Arn, Win, and Charles Arn. *Catch the Wave: A Handbook for Effective Ministry with Senior Adults.* Kansas City: Beacon Hill, 1999.

Beckner, W. Thomas, and Jeff Park, eds. *Effective Jail and Prison Ministry for the 21st Century.* Charlotte, NC: Coalition of Prison Evangelists (COPE), 1998.

Bowers, Curt. *Forward Edge of the Battle Area.* Kansas City: Beacon Hill, 1987.

Burkett, Larry. *Business by the Book.* Nashville: Thomas Nelson, 1998.

Chinula, Donald M. *Building King's Beloved Community: Foundations for Pastoral Care and Counseling with the Oppressed.* Cleveland, OH: United Church Press, 1997.

Clinebell, Howard. *Basic Types of Pastoral Care and Counseling.* New Haven: Yale University, 1983.

Covent, Henry. *Ministry to the Incarcerated.* Chicago: Loyola Press, 1995.

Everly, George, and Jeff Mitchell. *Critical Incident Stress Management.* 2nd ed. Elliott City: Chevron, 1999.

Federation of Fire Chaplains Training Manual, http://www.firechaplains.org.

Figley, Charles. *Compassion Fatigue.* Elliott City: Chevron, 1994.

Fitchett, George. *Assessing Spiritual Needs.* Minneapolis: Augsburg Fortress, 1993.

Friedman, Dayle, ed. *Jewish Pastoral Care: A Practical Handbook from Traditional and Contemporary Sources.* 2nd ed. Woodstock, VT: Jewish Lights, 2000.

Hiltner, Seward. *Pastoral Counseling.* Nashville: Abingdon, 1949.

Holst, Lawrence E., ed. *Hospital Ministry: The Role of the Chaplain Today.* New York: Crossroad, 1990.

Hunter, Rodney J., and Nancy J. Ramsay, eds. *Dictionary of Pastoral Care and Counseling.* Nashville: Abingdon, 2005.

Kirkwood, Neville A. *Pastoral Care to Muslims: Building Bridges.* Binghamton, NY: Haworth Press, 2002.

————— *I Love a Cop: What Police Families Need to Know.* New York: Guilford Press, 2000.

Kirschman, Ellen. *I Love A Fire Fighter: What the Family Needs to Know.* New York: The Guilford Press, 2004.

Labcqz, Karen. *Ethics and Spiritual Care: A Guide for Pastors, Chaplains, and Spiritual Directors.* Nashville: Abingdon, 2000.

Lartey, Emmanuel Y. *In Living Color: An Intercultural Approach to Pastoral Care and Counseling.* With a foreword by James Newton Poling. London: Jessica Kingsley, 2003.

Lewis-Herman, Judith. *Trauma and Recover.* New York: Basic Books, 1992.

McCormick, Jan. "There Is No Such Thing as a Resistant Client," *Marriage and Family: A Christian Journal* 5, no. 1 (2002):

Moessner, Jeanne Stevenson. *A Primer in Pastoral Care.* Creative Pastoral Care and Counseling Series. Minneapolis: Augsburg Fortress, 2005.

Montilla, R. Esteban. *Pastoral Care and Counseling with Latino/as.* Creative Pastoral Care and Counseling. Minneapolis: Augsburg Fortress, 2006.

Mullis, David E., Sr. "Business and Industrial Chaplaincy: The Chaplain's Ministry Plan." D.Min. diss., Regent University, School of Divinity, 1999.

Normile, Patti. *Visiting the Sick*. Cincinnati: St Anthony Messinger, 1992.

Paget, Naomi. *Disaster Relief Chaplain Training Manual*. Alpharetta, GA: North American Mission Board of the Southern Baptist Convention, 2004.

Plummer, David B. "Chaplaincy: The Greatest Story Never Told," *The Journal of Pastoral Care* 50 (1996): 1–11.

Pruyser, Paul W. *The Minister as Diagnostician*. Philadelphia: Westminster, 1976.

Quick, Ellen K. *Doing What Works in Brief Therapy: A Strategic Solution Focused Approach*. San Diego: Academic Press, 1996.

Ramsay, Nancy J., ed. *Pastoral Care and Counseling: Redefining the Paradigms*. Nashville: Abingdon, 2005.

Ramsay, Nancy J. *Pastoral Diagnosis: A Resource for Ministries of Care and Counseling*. Minneapolis: Augsburg Fortress, 1998.

Wimberly, Edward P. *African American Pastoral Care*. Nashville: Abingdon, 1991.

The Work of the Chaplain is the latest addition to the best-selling "Work of the Church" Series.

With over 900,000 copies sold in the series, it's in good company!

Available "Work of" titles include:

The Church Business Meeting R. Dale Merrill 978-0-8170-0409-5 $9.00

The Church Newsletter Handbook Clayton A. Lord Jr. 978-0-8170-1264-9 $15.00

Church Officers at Work, Revised Edition Glenn H. Asquith 978-0-8170-0048-6 $9.00

Work of the Church: Getting the Job Done in Boards and Committees David R. Sawyer 978-0-8170-1116-1 $9.00

The Work of the Church Treasurer, Revised Edition Thomas E. McLeod 978-0-8170-1189-5 $13.00

The Work of the Church Trustee Orlando L. Tibbetts 978-0-8170-0825-3 $10.00

The Work of the Clerk, New Edition M. Ingrid Dvirnak 978-0-8170-1253-3 $8.00

The Work of the Deacon and Deaconess Harold Nichols 978-0-8170-0328-9 $10.00

The Work of the Pastor Victor D. Lehman 978-0-8170-1473-5 $12.00

Work of the Pastoral Relations Committee Emmett V. Johnson 978-0-8170-0984-7 $11.00

The Work of the Sunday School Superintendent Idris W. Jones, Revised by Ruth L. Spencer 978-0-8170-1229-8 $10.00

The Work of the Usher Alvin D. Johnson 978-0-8170-0356-2 $8.00

The Work of the Worship Committee Linda Bonn 978-0-8170-1294-6 $9.00

NOW AVAILABLE IN SETS!

■ Complete library… includes first 13 books in the series! 978-0-8170-1847-2 $99.00

■ The five-book set includes our most popular titles: *The Work of Deacon and Deaconess, The Work of the Usher, The Work of the Sunday School Superintendent, The Work of the Church Trustee*, and *The Work of the Pastor.* 978-0-8170-1488-9 $37.00

Order online at www.judsonpress.com, or call 800-458-3766.

JUDSON PRESS

3 4711 00185 8333

RS SINCE 1824